DEDICATION

To all the saints within this book:
I pray I made you real.

Saints of the Seasons for Children

Ethel Marbach Pochocki

ST. ANTHONY MESSENGER PRESS

Cincinnati, Ohio

Nihil Obstat:
> Rev. Hilarion Kistner, O.F.M.
> Rev. John J. Jennings

Imprimi Potest:
> Rev. Jeremy Harrington, O.F.M.
> Provincial

Imprimatur:
> +Daniel E. Pilarczyk, V.G.
> Archdiocese of Cincinnati
> July 31, 1979; January 10, 1980;
> May 22, 1980; July 14, 1981

All Scripture passages in italic are taken from *The New American Bible*, copyright ©1970 by the Confraternity of Christian Doctrine, and are used by permission. All rights reserved. All other Scripture passages are paraphrase.

Cover design by Julie Lonneman and Mary Alfieri
Book design, cover and inside illustrations by Julie Lonneman

ISBN 0-86716-319-4

A Word to Parents and Teachers

Children live in close touch with the seasons. Only a few years have been marked in their memories; they are still surprised by the miracle of spring, the hush of falling snow, autumn's glorious blaze of color. Wise teachers and parents build on this wonder to teach the structure of time that encloses human life and history, to teach young voices songs in praise of the Creator.

We who believe that Jesus Christ is Lord of time, Lord of life and history, also mark the seasonal rhythms of the Church year. The revision of the Roman calendar mandated by Vatican II had a twofold purpose: to put believers into closer touch with the changing seasons of the Paschal Mystery and to dramatize the sweep of human holiness across centuries and national boundaries in commemorating the saints.

Ethel Marbach's *Saints of the Seasons for Children* allows youngsters entry into the mysteries of both calendars. From the great liturgical seasons of Lent and Easter, Advent and Christmas, the author draws the biblical figures who people the Sunday readings into the company of Christian saints associated with the seasonal events. From the rich stretches of ordinary time she chooses a representative sample of saints great and small and weaves their stories into the seasons of the year. With warmth and humor she brings them all to life—people who are just like her young readers in their human struggles, people who are like none of us in the holiness they have achieved.

This volume includes under one cover what previously appeared as four separate titles: *Saints-in-Waiting* (Advent/Christmastide); *Saints Budding Everywhere* (Winter/Spring); *Saints for the Journey* (Lent/Easter); *Saints at Harvest-Time* (Autumn). That means 49 stories for independent reading, classroom or family discussion and liturgical use—more than one a week for the school year!

Although some of the saints included have feasts which fall in the summer months, many important figures from that season are not included in these volumes developed specifically for the *school* year. For easy cross-referencing, however, all the saints with spring or summer feasts included in other seasonal collections are listed in the Contents under More Saints Budding Everywhere (Spring/Summer). For example, St. Thomas' feast day is July 3, but his journey from doubt to belief is included in the Lent/Easter collection of Saints for the Journey.

The introduction to each seasonal collection—also written for children—provides insight into the author's reasons for choosing particular saints for that season.

Contents

Saints-in-Waiting

Advent/Christmastide

This is an assortment of *before* and *after* saints. There are those who wondered about God's promised Son *before* he was Jesus, who knew him only as the Messiah who would come from heaven to save them. And there are those who knew him *after* he came to earth as Jesus and lived for 33 years in a specific time and place. They are saints "after the fact." They know whom they are following and why.

These people come from both Old and New Testament to take their places in the Advent liturgy. They sit in the pews, patiently waiting for the drama to begin, a mixed group. The writers, John and Luke, put their heads together and weigh their words with pursed lips. Nicholas' pockets bulge with hard candy and clatter against the wood. John the Baptist sits at the back because his hair isn't combed. The Holy Innocents sit in the front row waiting for the cake.

On the other side are those holy ones of the Old Testament, Ruth and David and Isaiah and the rest, who sit in the dark and see only with the eyes of faith. They have been promised a Messiah and so they sit and wait. What would be his size or shape or color God did not specify. His prophets have posted signs and portents along the way: *Believe; Don't Believe; Watch for This; Beware of That;* and the dreams and prophecies of these honored ones have been heeded as the Word of God himself.

This, then, is a gathering together of lives which have been caught up in the Christmas story: saints-in-waiting, clustered about in the dark of centuries, hushed and expectant till that moment when the spark will catch and the Light will shine forth for all the world to see.

Ruth

here was once a good woman named Naomi who, with her husband, Elimelech, and their two sons, had to leave their home in Bethlehem because of a great famine. All Israel was bare of food. Trees were shriveled and dry and brown, and the cows were so thin their ribs showed through their hides.

So, along with a great many other people, they left Israel. They settled in another land called Moab, where they built a home and began a new life among people who were not Jews as they were—people who prayed to fat stone idols instead of to God.

Their sons grew up and married, and Naomi loved both their wives deeply. They had a happy life together for 10 years, but then it was saddened by the deaths of all three husbands.

Naomi and Orpah and Ruth, her daughters-in-law, were now widows. Without her husband Naomi was very lonely in Moab and she felt a longing to return to her home in Bethlehem. She had heard news at the marketplace that Israel was once again a land bursting with the good things of life. The fields of corn and barley were ripe and full, and the fig and olive trees heavy with fruit. Naomi decided to return to her country to live the rest of her life with her friends and family, if any were left.

She called her two daughters-in-law to her and kissed them good-bye tenderly. "Go," she said, "return each of you to your mother's house. May the Lord be as kind to you as you have been to me."

Both the young women cried, for they truly loved Naomi as a mother. Orpah hugged her tightly and vowed she would think of her each night as she blew out her candle and watched the smoke rise to heaven, praying that she would be well and happy. And she left, wiping her tears with her veil.

Ruth, however, would not leave. She clung to Naomi and said, "Do not ask me to leave you. It is no use to tell me to stay here. Moab is no longer my home. Wherever you go, I will go, and where you stop, I will stop. Your people shall be my people, and your God my God. Where you die, I shall die, and there I will be buried. Nothing but death shall part you from me."

Naomi said gently, "Your sister-in-law has gone back to her people and her gods. You must go, too."

"No," said Ruth, "I have always obeyed you in all things but this. I will not leave you."

Naomi shook her head, but in her heart she was touched to be so loved by this young woman. So the two of them set off for Bethlehem and reached the city at the beginning of harvest time. The fields were filled with corn and barley ready to be gathered into the granaries for food for the winter. Naomi thought there might be enough left when the workers were through for them to glean, that is, take what remained on the ground.

She remembered a cousin of a cousin who owned the fields, a man of great wealth called Boaz, and asked permission of his workers to gather up the barley. The workers saw no harm in this, so the two women set to work filling their bags.

But Naomi was frail and could not stand the hot sun, so Ruth told her to sit and rest under the cedar trees and smell their sweet fragrance while she quickly gathered enough for both of them.

Ruth worked long until the afternoon sun turned from gold to pink and then purple. Boaz, who had come to check up on his workers, came upon the young woman with surprise. She was bending over, sweeping the grain into her bag with her hands, and she jumped

3

up, startled, when he said, "The Lord be with you."

"The Lord bless you," she replied quickly, a bit frightened because she did not know who he was.

Boaz whispered to his servant, standing by with a jug of water for his master, "Who is that young girl, and what is she doing here?" The servant explained that she had come back with Naomi from the land of Moab and had asked permission to glean the fields for food.

"Are you thirsty, young woman?" he asked kindly. Ruth nodded yes because her throat was so dry, and she had been wishing for a nice cool drink.

"Please feel free to drink from this vessel. It is yours." Ruth bowed low and thanked him, and then took a cup of the water to Naomi before taking some for herself.

"Will you come here tomorrow?" Boaz asked.

"Yes, sir, if there is still barley to be found. I don't want to be greedy—but it will be good to have for the winter," said Ruth.

The next day Ruth returned and was amazed to find many piles of barley still untouched in the field. How could she have missed all this yesterday! She didn't know that Boaz had secretly come in the early morning hours and scattered the grain on purpose.

That evening, Ruth showed three bags full to Naomi, who was also surprised at the amount. Ruth told her then about the kindness of Boaz, and Naomi sighed and smiled. "Blessed is he that took notice of you. May the Lord bless him, for the Lord has not stopped showing kindness to the living and the dead."

Ruth continued to work in the fields of Boaz and he told all his workers and servants to watch over and protect her from any harm. When she found out all he had been doing for her she came to him and said, with tears in her eyes, "Why have I found favor with you when I am only a stranger in your land?"

Boaz took her hand and answered, "I have heard all that you have done for Naomi, my kin, and how you have left your father and mother and your land and have come to a people you have never known. May the Lord repay your good deeds and may a full reward be given you by the Lord God of Israel, under whose wings you have come to rest."

When the harvest season was over, Boaz went to the gate of the city where the ruling elders sat and made decisions and, according to Jewish custom, announced that he wanted to marry Ruth. Everyone thought this was a wonderful idea, for although she had been born in a different land, Ruth was such a courageous and loyal person, it made no matter at all.

And so they were married and had a son, whom they called Obed, who was the joy of his grandmother Naomi's life. When Obed grew up and married, he had a son named Jesse, and Jesse one day became the father of David.

Since Mary, our Lord's mother, is descended from David, we say that Jesus sprang from "the root of Jesse" and is of the House of David. Even though he had a heavenly Father, he also had parents and grandparents and great-great-way-back-in-the-olden-days ancestors on earth, just as you do.

How pleased Ruth must be to know that her loving heart and fearless trust in God's will was passed on through the centuries to her divine descendant!

David

nce upon a time there lived a very wise and respected prophet named Samuel who made a mistake. It may not seem like a mistake to us today, but to him it was a real whopper. You see, in those times everyone in Israel listened to Samuel, because *he* listened to God and gave Israel his messages.

Even though Samuel was a leader, the people wanted more. They wanted a real king and felt it was time that they have one, someone to lead them out of war and into a time of peace. So they went to Samuel and asked whom he would choose.

Samuel didn't think it was a very good idea at all, but he listened to what the Lord had to say and it seemed to him that the Lord agreed with the people. After some hesitation, Samuel chose Saul, a tall handsome daredevil. Saul lived on his nerve and was a jumpy sort of person. If you ate dinner with him around, your stomach was bound to get tied up in knots.

Saul was a good leader and he could be very kind and loving when he was in a good mood, but Samuel worried over how and where he was leading the Israelites. And Saul's moods got worse. After years of always having his own way, something happened inside Saul's mind. He couldn't bear to have anyone say no to him. If he wanted purple grapes served on scarlet glass plates and got green grapes on Blue Willow dishes instead, he went into such a rage he smashed all the dishes and the grapes as well.

Then he would become dizzy and everything would go black. All he could see as he fell to the ground were little flashes of stars, like fireflies on a summer's night. Afterwards he would say that an evil spirit had gotten into him.

Samuel's heart grieved that Saul acted so and that he, Samuel, had made such a mistake. The Lord spoke to him gently: "How long will you mourn for Saul, Samuel? Come, fill your horn with oil and go to find Jesse of Bethlehem, for I have chosen a king from among his sons."

Samuel always did as he was told by the Lord, but he was fearful that Saul would not be pleased if he thought he was about to be replaced. He asked the Lord, "How can I? If Saul finds out, he will kill me."

The Lord, as always, had a plan. He told Samuel to take a calf and go to Jesse's house to make a sacrifice to the Lord, as they did in those days. And then he would tell him which of Jesse's sons to anoint.

So Samuel did just that. Jesse was honored that such a wise man had chosen his house for a sacrifice, and being a polite host, he began to introduce his eight sons to his guest.

First came Eliab, who was so tall and golden in appearance Samuel thought it must be he who would be the chosen one. But the Lord said, "Do not be so impressed by his good looks. I do not see as you see. People only look at outward appearances, but the Lord looks deep into the heart."

Next came Abinadab. "Keep going," said the Lord.

What about Shammah? "Three down," said the Lord.

One by one, seven of Jesse's sons met Samuel and although all of them were good young men, none of them made his heart quicken.

"Are these all your children, Jesse?" he asked. Jesse frowned and scratched his head and then his face lit up with a smile.

Yes, there was another—his youngest, David, who was out in the hills tending the sheep.

"Please fetch him," asked Samuel, who was getting weary. But when David stood before him, young and rosy and glowing with health, he forgot his impatience and he knew this was the boy. "Arise, anoint him, for this is the one," said God to Samuel.

So Samuel took him to a nearby hill, filled his horn with sweet olive oil mixed with incense, and poured it upon David's curly red hair. And the spirit of the Lord was with David, the next king of Israel, from that day on.

Neither David nor Samuel said anything of this to anyone. David went back to tending his sheep. It was here in the hills of Bethlehem that the young shepherd grew in love for God and all his creation. Nothing escaped his eye and heart: the shades of green in the pastures, the golden shine of grain bending in the wind, the music of water running over rocks. His joy overflowed and he could not contain it. He played his lyre (a small harp he could rest on his shoulder and hold in his lap) and sang his own poems and danced barefoot around his sheep. The sound of his voice bounced off the hills and echoed into the village, and the women would stop grinding their corn or beating their wet clothes on rocks to bask in the pure sweetness of the sound.

He grew also in strength and muscle as he spent his young years in the sun and rain and wind. He climbed cliffs and skipped rocks and practiced throwing stones in a homemade sling until he could hit perfectly the target which his mind had ordered. This skill came in handy whenever his sheep were attacked by lions or bears, which they sometimes were.

David would take aim and knock them down with a single rock shot from his sling, run up and rescue his lambs from the very jaws of the wild beasts. He knew that alone he could not do this, that God had given him the courage. So he would kneel down with the lamb still in his arms and pour out his thanks in yet another song of praise. He never forgot that whenever he needed it, God would give him the strength to do what was right, no matter how impossible or frightening it might seem.

Men needed lots of courage in those days. There were always

wars and killings and very little of "the peace of the Lord" to go around. The Israelites, led by Saul, had one particular enemy they especially feared and hated, the Philistines.

At this time, when David was still skipping rocks, the Philistines felt they had the edge over the Israelites. They bragged they could lick the Israelites blindfolded and walking backwards because they had something no one else had: a *giant*.

He was *really* a giant, all nine feet, nine inches of him. His name was Goliath and he came from Gath. He was as mean as he was big. He knew he could have anything he wanted, because who wanted to stop him? The Philistines treated him very carefully. After all, he was a dangerous weapon, one who could turn on them as easily as he did on their enemies.

Goliath held the Israelites in fear and he knew it. He would walk up and down his mountain (across from the Israelites' camp) and cause the boulders to fall and trees to tremble at their roots. And when he laughed his mean, raspy hot-breathed laugh, he blew the leaves off the trees and the fresh wash off the clotheslines.

During one particular battle, the Philistines sat on one hill and the Israelites on another, with a deep valley between them. For 40 days, nothing happened. The giant would come out and call, with a sneer in his voice, "Well, you lily-livered servants of Saul! Is there none of you brave enough to do battle with the great Goliath? Who will fight me hand to hand?" And he would roar with laughter because he knew not even the bravest of soldiers wanted to take him on. Even the tallest would just come up to the giant's bellybutton, and he could pick him up and squash him between his hands like a fly.

"Listen," he yelled, "if anyone can kill me, then the Philistines will give up and become your servants. If I kill one of you, then you will submit to us. Isn't that fair enough?" And he roared again, his spiked helmet glinting in the sun, and he waved a spear so enormous it would take five ordinary men to carry it.

Now David, who had been sent by his father to bring cheese and bread and wine to his brothers in the army, listened to Goliath and

watched him striding up and down the hill, crunching little pine trees under his huge feet.

He called out, "Here I am, Goliath, I will fight you!"

Everyone laughed at the young boy, so eager, so certain that he could beat the giant. But he persisted so long they finally brought him before Saul, who also smiled at the idea of this shepherd doing battle with Goliath.

Saul already knew David and loved him. His servants had brought him to play for the king when he had his black moods, because music was the one thing which would soothe him and take away his headaches. David would play his harp and remind Saul that the Lord who took care of sheep and green meadows and still waters would take care of him, too. And Saul would weep and embrace him, refreshed in

10

both body and soul. So David would come and play for the king whenever he called and then return home to his family at night.

Now Saul did not want to lose him to this monster of a giant. "You are just a boy, my son, and a gentle poet at that. Even my soldiers, hardened men, will not risk their lives for such folly."

David would not give up. He knew that with God by his side he could do anything. "I have fought lions and bears and, with God's help, have won over the wild beasts. Goliath is no worse. Please let me try!"

Saul finally gave in. He insisted that David wear the royal armor, but it was so large and so heavy, David asked politely please to let him fight in his own clothes and his own way. He put his shepherd's tunic back on and his sandals, slung his bag over his shoulder, and went down to the stream in the valley. He carefully chose five smooth stones of just the right size and weight and slipped them into his leather bag. Then he took his sling, a long strip of worn leather, and put that also into his bag. Armed with these five stones, his sling, and his trust in God, David went forth to meet Goliath.

"Here I come, Goliath!" he yelled across the valley to the giant. At first, Goliath could not believe his eyes when he saw this little ant of a human coming down the mountain to meet him. No armor, no helmet, a staff instead of a spear, just a young boy with red curly hair, singing and dancing a bit in time to the music.

The giant grew very angry. They were making fun of him, sending such a joke to fight him.

"Am I a dog," he bellowed, "that they send this boy, this worm, to fight me? I will give his body to the birds of the air and the beasts of the field!"

"You there, Goliath," shouted back David, "you come with a sword and spear and shield, but I come to you in the name of the Lord of Hosts, the God of the armies of Israel!"

Quickly David took one of his stones from his bag and raised his sling. He took careful aim and slung it. It struck the giant right smack in the middle of his forehead. The giant fell with a tremendous noise in a crumpled heap at David's feet.

There were cries of fear and disbelief in the camp of the Philistines, and they took no time in fleeing their mountain, for they did not want to submit to the Israelites, no matter what the giant had said.

David knelt down on the spot and again gave thanks to God for being with him all the days of his life.

The young shepherd became Saul's favorite and came to live in his house. He married the king's daughter, Michal, and when Saul died, David became the king of Israel. He grew a curly red beard to match his hair and was a handsome sight, this leader anointed of the Lord. Even when he was king, he played his harp and kept on writing those beautiful songs we call the Psalms, and when he danced—how he loved to dance!—it was as though he were on fire with his love for God.

In one Psalm, he tells us to:

Praise the LORD in his sanctuary,
  praise him in the firmament of his strength.
Praise him for his mighty deeds,
  praise him for his sovereign majesty.
Praise him with the blast of the trumpet,
  praise him with lyre and harp,
Praise him with timbrel and dance,
  praise him with strings and pipe.
Praise him with sounding cymbals,
  praise him with clanging cymbals.
Let everything that has breath
  praise the LORD! Alleluia. (Ps 150:1-6)

And with every breath of his being, that is what David did. He made his life one big hymn of praise. Samuel must have felt satisfied that he didn't make a mistake, after all. It had been part of God's plan that good come out of bad, that because of Saul, there was David, and out of David came Mary, and through Mary, God gave us Jesus.

All things worked to the good!

Isaiah

ong before Jesus was born, there was a prophet called Isaiah who was not very popular with the people of Israel. You'd think they would like having a prophet around. It would be very handy to know if you would be having unexpected company for dinner on Thursday or if Aunt Carol will have a baby girl in October.

But you'd also have to know about the unhappy things that lay ahead, for it was a prophet's job, since he spoke for God, to give all messages, good or bad. Since most of what Isaiah saw for Israel was not good, he annoyed the people, and then depressed them. Sometimes they listened to him, but more often they did not. They did not like to hear laments and threats of wars and punishments. It was hard enough to take care of daily troubles without worrying over tomorrow's destruction.

But now and then among his warnings, Isaiah sprinkled joyful words which brought hope to the Jews. The composer George Frederick Handel wrote glorious music to one prophecy, which he called *The Messiah*. You will usually hear it at Christmas:

> *The people who walked in darkness*
> *have seen a great light;*
> *Upon those who dwelt in the land of gloom*
> *a light has shown.*

14

For a child is born to us, a son is given us;
  upon his shoulder dominion rests.
They name him Wonder-Counselor, God-Hero,
  Father-Forever, Prince of Peace.
His dominion is vast
  and forever peaceful,
From David's throne, and over his kingdom,
  which he confirms and sustains
By judgment and justice,
  both now and forever. (Isaiah 9:1-2, 5-6)

Isaiah told of Christ's coming in another prophecy, and his words sparked the imagination of an American artist, Edward Hicks, many centuries later. He created a painting called "The Peaceable Kingdom" (you may even have a copy of it hanging on your wall). In it the child Jesus is surrounded by all manner of wild animals lying at his feet and behaving themselves politely. These are the words which inspired the artist:

But a shoot shall sprout from the stump of Jesse,
  and from his roots a bud shall blossom.
The spirit of the LORD shall rest upon him:
  a spirit of wisdom and of understanding,
A spirit of counsel and of strength,
  a spirit of knowledge and of fear of the LORD ....
Not by appearance shall he judge,
  nor by hearsay shall he decide,
But he shall judge the poor with justice,
  and decide aright for the land's afflicted ....
Then the wolf shall be a guest of the lamb,
  and the leopard shall lie down with the kid;
The calf and the young lion shall browse together,
  with a little child to guide them.
The cow and the bear shall be neighbors,

together their young shall rest;
the lion shall eat hay like the ox....
There shall be no harm or ruin on all my holy mountain;
for the earth shall be filled with knowledge of the LORD,
as water covers the sea. (Isaiah 11:1-4, 6-7, 9)

We can't really call Isaiah the Prophet of Gloom and Doom. He knew that no matter how dark the days ahead, there would always be a Light for us to follow, one which would never go out because of wind or rain or lack of power. He said:

Sing praise to the LORD for his glorious achievement;
let this be known throughout all the earth.
Shout with exultation, O city of Zion,
for great in your midst
is the Holy One of Israel! (Isaiah 12:5-6)

I wouldn't be a bit surprised if he even smiled as he rejoiced!

16

The Immaculate Conception

 very long time ago, God decided that he would send his Son, Jesus, to live on earth with us and show us how we might share heaven with him and the angels and the saints and everyone who had ever loved God enough to be there.

Because Jesus would be a very special human being, his mother would also have to be very special. She would be God's bridge from heaven to earth. Most of our mothers are special, but our Lord's mother would have to be even better. The very best.

She would have to be the kind of mother who never gets angry or impatient or spanks before she hears your story. And even if she were tired or her legs ached, she couldn't go into her bedroom and slam the door and tell you to go away.

She would have to be patient, understanding, wise, cheerful, thrifty, brave, joyful, generous, and trust God with all her heart. She would know what her life would be as the mother of God's Son on earth, and she would accept it quietly in her heart.

This sounds terribly hard for any person, for none of us is born perfect—none of us except Mary. God chose her and her parents very carefully. He picked Ann and Joachim, an elderly couple who had prayed for years for God to send them a child.

He rewarded them for their faith by sending a daughter, whom they called Mary. God told them she was the one person in the world who had not one shadow of a sin on her soul. Because she was the one chosen to be Jesus' mother, she was perfect, wrapped in God's grace.

In the Canticles (or Song of Songs) of the Bible, there are lovely words which have for centuries made Christians think of the moment Mary's soul came into life. She is one who "came forth as the morning, rising fair as the moon, bright as the sun, shining in the temple of God as the morning star in the midst of a cloud."

Mary is our Morning Star. She is also the Immaculate Conception. *Immaculate* means absolutely pure, untouched by sin, without spot or stain, like the first snow on your doorstep in the morning before you walk on it. *Conception* is what happens when you make an idea—a poem, an apple pie, a baby—become real.

Mary, the Immaculate Conception, was born nine months after this day, in September. From that time, not only Jesus, but all of us, have had a perfectly real, loving Mother.

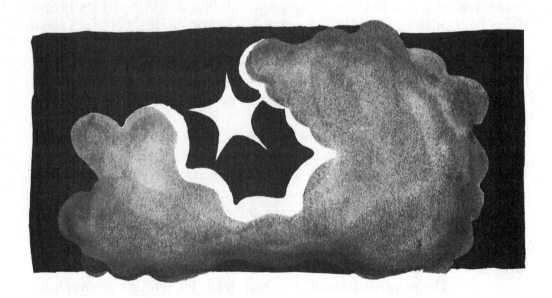

Elizabeth and Zechariah

nce upon a time, there lived an elderly couple named Elizabeth and Zechariah, who "walked in the way of the Lord," as the Bible says. They were good, honest people who followed all the commandments and laws of the Jewish religion, and the Lord was good to them in return.

They were content with their lives, except for the fact that they had no children. They never complained, but in their hearts they felt a quiet sadness that they would never know the joy of being parents. They were quite old now, and there was no hope that they would ever have a child, so they tried not to think about it. They put all their energy into doing whatever else God wanted them to do.

Zechariah was a priest of the Levite tribe and one of his duties was to see that incense on the altar was lit at the right time and burnt in the right manner. One day the smoke from the incense rose straight up into one large cloud, and in the center of it appeared an angel in robes of gold and scarlet and shimmering royal blue.

Zechariah was terribly frightened and wondered what he had done wrong. But the angel said, *"Do not be frightened, Zechariah; your prayer has been heard. Your wife Elizabeth shall bear a son whom you shall name John. Joy and gladness will be yours, and many will rejoice at his birth; for he will be great in the eyes of the Lord .... He will be filled with the Holy Spirit from his mother's womb .... God himself will go before him . . . , to turn the hearts of fathers to their children and the rebellious to the wisdom of the just, and to prepare for the Lord a people well disposed"* (Luke 1:13-15, 17).

The angel told Zechariah that John was to be the forerunner of Jesus, someone who would prepare the way for him. Poor Zechariah! This was all too much for him to understand. First, that he and Elizabeth would have a baby—impossible! Then that he would be the forerunner of the Messiah—just as impossible!

But God didn't ask him to understand. He just asked him to trust him. But Zechariah didn't have that kind of faith. He asked the angel for a sign so he could believe. "You must understand, I don't really believe this is happening," he said to the angel, "even though I am standing here talking to you. It can't be. My wife and I are too old to have a child. How can I believe what you say is true?"

The angel said firmly, "My name is Gabriel. I am a spirit of the highest order who stands in the presence of God, and the Lord has sent me to announce these good tidings. Because you cannot believe, you shall be unable to speak until all the things I have told you come to pass."

Zechariah went home in awe and fear. No matter how hard he tried, no words would come from his mouth.

"Zechariah, what is wrong?" exclaimed Elizabeth when she saw his pale face and shaking hands.

He called for a tablet and a pencil and wrote down what had happened. Elizabeth read and rejoiced. There was no doubt in her mind. *She* believed. "The Lord has dealt with me," she said, and she busied herself getting ready for this incredibly special child.

For nine months, Zechariah spoke not one word. He filled pages and pages of paper with his everyday conversation. In time, a baby boy was born to Elizabeth and everyone in the family rejoiced. A fine son to carry on his father's name, everyone smiled.

"You will call him Zechariah, of course, after his father," they said to Elizabeth.

"No," said she, "his name shall be John."

"Oh, no, you can't do that. Why none of your kin bear that name. Wherever did you get the name John?"

Elizabeth turned to Zechariah and asked him what the child's name should be. Zechariah wrote on his pad, "John is his name." Suddenly his tongue was untied. His lips moved and he began to praise God out loud.

Such rejoicing could not be contained within the small house in the hills of Judea. It spread through the neighboring villages until everyone wondered, "What shall this child be, for surely the hand of God is upon him!"

Zechariah, filled with the Holy Spirit and enjoying the sound of his own voice again, began to sing this hymn:

Blessed be the Lord the God of Israel
  because he has visited and ransomed his people.
And you, O child, shall be called
  prophet of the Most High;
For you shall go before the Lord
  to prepare straight paths for him,
Giving his people a knowledge of salvation
  in freedom from their sins.
All this is the work of the kindness of our God;
  he, the Dayspring, shall visit us in his mercy
To shine on those who sit in darkness
  and in the shadow of death,
  to guide our feet into the way of peace. (Luke 1:68, 76-79)

And that is exactly what John, who ran ahead to make a path for our Lord, did.

9ハ3 / 95
Dec 1999

John the Baptist

ong ago in Jesus' time, there lived a strange young man who made his home alone in the desert hill-country of Judea. We don't think of him as strange today because we know him as John, the son of Elizabeth and Zechariah, and the forerunner and cousin of Jesus. But to the people of his time who lived in his village, he was certainly a strange one.

He was not an old hermit who, having lived a full life, decided to finish his days praying and fasting on a spot of parched earth. No, John was a young man in his 20's when he made the desert his home. He let his hair grow long and ate only locusts (dead, I imagine) and wild honey which the bees had hidden for him in the rocky cliffs. He wore only the skins of animals.

Why he chose to wait for our Lord in this manner is a secret between him and God. Perhaps it was to make true the words of the prophet Isaiah, who told us to listen to the message of someone crying out:

> *In the desert prepare the way of the Lord!*
>   *Make straight in the wasteland a highway*
>   *for our God!*
> *Every valley shall be filled in,*
>   *every mountain and hill shall be made low;*

23

The rugged land shall be made a plain,
*   the rough country, a broad valley.*
*Then the glory of the L*ORD *shall be revealed,*
*   and all mankind shall see it together . . . .(Isaiah 40:3-5)*

John wanted to be by himself while he waited for our Lord, but because he dressed and lived in such a different way, people who lived around the desert became curious. They went to see for themselves. John began preaching to them about the Messiah and how they must get ready for him by cleansing their souls and bodies in the River Jordan. This would be their baptism into a new life.

He didn't mean just a light sprinkling over the head, the way the priest may have baptized you. He meant every part of you was dipped deep down under the water so no spot, not even behind your ears or between your toes, would miss being cleansed. So too, he said, would the

sorrow for your sins spread to every corner of your soul, and their stains would disappear.

Some began to praise him and say that *he* was the Messiah, but he told them, "I baptize you with water, but there is one who is mightier. He will baptize you with the Holy Spirit and fire!"

This one would be the Messiah. John's job was to run before him, as heralds announced kings, with trumpets and cries, bidding all make clear the royal way. With baptism, John cleared away the garbage that cluttered the path. With his preaching, he pressed the people to repent of their old ways and to do good in Christ's name.

"Let him who has two coats give to him who has none," he said, "and let him who has food share it with those who are hungry."

One day, a few months later, a large crowd of fishermen and shepherds and housewives and tax collectors came to the Jordan to be baptized. One man in a white robe caught John's eye. John looked at him long and deeply, and the man returned his gaze with love.

John knew instantly that this man was Jesus. Although they were cousins of the same age, they had grown up apart and did not know each other. But there was no doubt in John's heart at all that here standing in the crowd was the Messiah.

Jesus came up to John and asked to be baptized, and John, too startled to be his usual fiery self, said meekly, "It is *I* who ought to be baptized by you."

"No," said Jesus, "you do it, to fulfill all the prophecies."

So John did, and when Jesus came up from under the water, a dove burst forth from the sky and rested over his head. A voice came out of heaven saying, "This is my dearly beloved Son, in whom I am well pleased!"

From that moment, it was clear that Jesus was not just a fine carpenter, the good son of Mary and Joseph, as he had been known in his home of Nazareth. He was God's Son, the long-awaited Messiah whose coming John had announced to the world.

Washed in the water of the River Jordan by John, Jesus had made himself known.

Luke

nce upon a time, there was a doctor who lived in Greece, a pagan who had never seen our Lord or known of him. He lived a happy life and was satisfied to continue it as a good Gentile until one night when he was caught up in a crowd listening to the apostle Paul preach. He changed his life in the blinking of an eye.

He joined Paul as his companion and fellow-worker, and often as his doctor. (Paul was often careless about what he ate—it could be sawdust for all he cared—and how he slept.) We know this good doctor now as Luke the Evangelist, who wrote one of the four Gospels of the New Testament. Matthew, Mark and John wrote the other three. Although each of them wrote the story of our Lord's life, each told the story a little differently.

This is to be expected, for each author was unique. It would be the same if four artists painted the same sunset. Can you imagine how different each sky would be?

Luke told his story in a very *meticulous* manner. You can almost tell by saying it what that word means: nitpicking! He was very careful about everything he wrote down. He never said *maybe,* or *perhaps,* or *it is said.*

He tells us right off, in the first verse, what his intentions are: "A lot of people has written about the wonderful things God has

27

done for us through his Son, Jesus—even people who saw the miracles and the crucifixion and talked to Jesus after he rose from the dead. I have looked over everything that has been written very carefully, and I have decided to write for you an *orderly* account.''

Luke must have been the kind of person you would like to have come to dinner. He was able to talk of so many things. Being a doctor, he could tell you about the herbs to use to stop a bleeding cut, or a bitter spring tonic to take to wake you up. He could tell if you were flushed from excitement or really had a fever.

Since some say he was also an artist, he could tell you about what is rumored to be his most famous work, a painting of Mary called The Black Madonna, or Our Lady of Czestochowa, which may be seen today at a shrine in Poland. *It is said* that Luke talked with Mary and knew her, so this haunting and lovely portrait may be a true image of her.

But the best conversation with this apostle would be listening to his telling of the first Christmas story. All over the world on Christmas Eve, Christians read Luke's story of our Lord's birth. Luke the writer and Luke the painter come together to create a warm and loving picture:

> *In those days Caesar Augustus published a decree ordering a census of the whole world. This first census took place while Quirinius was governor of Syria. Everyone went to register, each to his own town. And so Joseph went from the town of Nazareth in Galilee to Judea, to David's town of Bethlehem—because he was of the house and lineage of David—to register with Mary, his espoused wife, who was with child.*
>
> *While they were there, the days of her confinement were completed. She gave birth to her first-born son and wrapped him in swaddling clothes and laid him in a manger, because there was no room for them in the place where travelers lodged.*
>
> *There were shepherds in that locality, living in the fields and keeping night watch by turns over their flocks. The angel of the Lord appeared to them as the glory of the Lord shone around them, and they*

were very much afraid. The angel said to them: "You have nothing to fear! I come to proclaim good news to you—tidings of great joy to be shared by the whole people. This day in David's city a savior has been born to you, the Messiah and Lord. Let this be a sign to you: in a manger you will find an infant wrapped in swaddling clothes." Suddenly, there was with the angel a multitude of the heavenly host, praising God and saying,

"Glory to God in high heaven,
    peace on earth to those on whom his favor rests."

When the angels had returned to heaven, the shepherds said to one another: "Let us go over to Bethlehem and see this event which the Lord has made known to us." They went in haste and found Mary and Joseph, and the baby lying in the manger; once they saw, they understood what had been told them concerning this child. All who heard of it were astonished at the report given them by the shepherds.

Mary treasured all these things and reflected on them in her heart. The shepherds returned, glorifying and praising God for all they had heard and seen, in accord with what had been told them (Luke 2:1-20).

Simeon and Anna

nce upon a time in Jerusalem, there lived two very old and holy people named Simeon and Anna. They were very fragile and their bones were brittle, and they were not too steady on their feet. Anna's hair was white, what you could see from under her veil, and Simeon's white beard hung heavy and trailed to below his waist.

We put Simeon and Anna together in one story not because they were married or first cousins or because they even knew each other. They just happened to be together in the Temple, as part of God's plan, when Jesus was brought there by his parents to be presented.

It was the Jewish custom that a baby boy be presented at the Temple 40 days after he had been born. The parents were to bring a sacrifice in praise of the Lord: a lamb and a turtledove if they were rich; a pair of turtledoves or pigeons if they were poor.

Since Joseph and Mary did not own a lamb (they had only been *loaned* the Lamb of God), they brought two turtledoves in a round wicker basket. Joseph carried the cooing birds, while Mary held the child snugly in his thin blanket.

Now Simeon had been waiting for this morning all his life. He was a very just, honest and holy man who was known about the city as a scribe, or writer. The Lord often spoke to him, and Simeon was a good listener. He did what God wished without question. As a reward,

God told him that he would not die until he had actually seen the Son of God on earth. So he had been waiting and waiting.

This morning the Holy Spirit urged him to stop writing and go to the Temple. So Simeon put down his pen and went immediately, not knowing what to expect. He climbed the steps along with a couple and their baby. The young mother with the blue veil held the child tightly to her, so only his dark hair showed above the blanket. Her husband, an older man, seemed bowed down with backpack, food supplies, the basket of doves and a heavy walking stick.

At that moment, Simeon's heart felt filled to bursting. The Holy Spirit whispered to him, "Now, Simeon, *now* is the moment for which you have waited all your life. Behold this child, your Savior!"

Inside the Temple, Simeon bowed low and asked permission to hold the baby, and as he held him high over his head, he began to praise God and bless him and the child's parents. He sang a song known to us now as the Canticle of Simeon:

> *Now Master, you can dismiss your servant in peace;*
> *   you have fulfilled your word.*
> *For my eyes have witnessed your saving deed*
> *   displayed for all the peoples to see:*
> *A revealing light to the Gentiles,*
> *   the glory of your people Israel. (Luke 2:29-32)*

Then he looked at Mary with tenderness and some sadness. "Behold," he said, "this child is destined for greatness. He will bring salvation to many people, but many others will oppose him. And the sword of sorrow will pierce your own heart."

Mary listened quietly. She knew why her Son was here and that she had been chosen because she understood his mission and had the strength to share in it. Still, as she felt the tight grip of his small warm fingers pulling on her hair or touching her eyes, she wished she could avoid the fear and pain already settling into her heart.

In the Temple at this same time was a prophetess, Anna, to

whom God had given the gift of seeing ahead to what would be. She was 84 years old, a widow who spent her life in the Temple praying and fasting, day and night. She came forward, also excited by the Holy Spirit, and asked Mary if she might hold Jesus.

She smiled at the baby, who was still sleeping through all of this, and kissed him and proclaimed in a loud, high voice that here was the Divine Redeemer of the Jews who had come to save Israel. Right here in her arms!

Joseph and Mary marveled over this. Of course *they* knew Jesus was God's Son, but it was hard not being able to share this good news with everyone. And here were these two wise people who knew it without being told!

Simeon and Anna were like two wisps of pink cloud fading in the evening sky, promising a lovely day tomorrow.

The Magi

Epiphany

nce upon a time there were three kings who came out of the East to bring gifts to a baby in Bethlehem and then returned home and were never heard of again. If it weren't for the fact that the baby was Jesus, we might never have known anything about them at all.

These three kings were clothed in mystery. We don't even know if they were really kings. Some say they were *almost*-kings, or Magi. Magi were wise men who studied the stars and planets, interpreted dreams and predicted future happenings. Some say they were soothsayers, or magicians, who were held in great respect and had as much power as kings. Or they might have been learned priests of an Oriental religion.

We don't know exactly where they came from. Some say they came out of Persia or Babylon or Assyria or Arabia. Wherever they began, it was a long, long journey from there to Jerusalem.

And why did they come? Since they were astrologers, they knew that the star which appeared in the sky when Jesus was born was a marvelous happening. They could not chart it or explain it by any natural means. In their religion, anything as fantastic as the birth of a new star meant that a very important person had been born.

Since there were many Jews living in the East, especially Persia, the Magi must have heard of the promised Messiah, or King of the Jews, whom God would send to save them.

And who were they? According to a venerable Christian tradition, the oldest was Melchior, who was 60 years old, very frail and pale, with a long white beard. He had to be helped by two pages to get onto his camel.

Then there was Balthasar, a tall black man with full, heavy beard and deep dark eyes, about 40 years old. And the youngest was Gaspar, a young man of 20 years, with curly hair, no beard, and a rosy complexion.

For a year they studied and planned and prepared, and when everything in the sky and on earth was in perfect harmony, they set off on their journey with 1,000 attendants: cooks, doctors, grooms for the camels, and three little pages to carry their special gifts.

They followed the star, which blinked and sparkled with every color like a many-sided diamond in the sun. It went before them until it came to the home of the child in Bethlehem. The Magi knelt at Jesus' feet and offered their gifts.

Melchior gave him gold, because Jesus was King.

Balthasar gave him frankincense, a sweet-smelling incense, because Jesus was God.

Gaspar gave him myrrh, a herb used for healing, because Jesus was human.

They rested one night, and in the morning left. No mention is made of them again in the Gospels. It is most likely that they went back to their lands in the East to tell the incredible tale of the star and the babe and the wicked King Herod who wanted to kill the child because he was the King of the Jews.

We don't know what happened to them. It is said that the apostle Thomas baptized them when he went to Persia and India, so they might very well be saints. If so, nobody wrote it down as a positive fact.

What is important to know is that Melchior, Balthasar and Gaspar were men of power, learning, wealth and, possibly, royal blood. They traveled for three years, without thought of time or danger or discomfort, to humble themselves before Jesus and to bring him the best they had to offer.

I'm sure the saints welcomed them to their company. Certainly they did not come to heaven as strangers, for Christians have for hundreds of years remembered their visit to Bethlehem on the feast of Epiphany. Epiphany means "showing forth"; the three kings were the first to see the light of Christ showing forth to all the far corners of the earth.

The Holy Innocents

nce upon a time on a December day in Bethlehem, something very sad happened because someone very wonderful had been born on Christmas Day. Twenty-five children, little boys two years old and younger, were killed by an incredibly evil king named Herod.

When someone is incredibly evil, we try to understand how he became that way. But Herod was *so* bad (he even killed four of his own sons), perhaps we had best leave him to God to figure out. I certainly would not like to be in *his* sandals on Judgment Day.

But we do wonder what kind of person could take the lives of these Holy Innocents, as they are called, who hadn't even had time to learn to be bad. *Innocents* are those who can do no wrong or harm because they don't know what they are doing.

Yet Herod was afraid of one such child who would take his throne and then Herod would no longer be King. Already three kings had arrived at his palace, traveling from a country in the East, asking, "Where is he that is born King of the Jews? For we have seen his star in the East and have come to worship him."

This made the King terribly nervous. He was impressed with their kingly robes and servants and mysterious jeweled boxes which he suspected held presents for someone royal.

Herod called together his wise men and fortune-tellers and asked them where this baby, this new King, had been born. And they told him, "In Bethlehem." So Herod thought up a clever plan.

He called the Magi into his living room and offered them cigars and chocolate-covered mints and said he hoped they would have a pleasant journey to Bethlehem.

"Oh, and by the way," he added quickly, "When you find this young child, please come back and bring me news of him, so I may go and worship him also."

The three kings followed their star to the stable and gave their gifts to Jesus and Mary. They spent the night in a cave nearby since the stable was already so crowded. In their dreams that night, an angel warned each of them that Herod was not to be trusted and wanted to kill the Infant King. So they took a different road home the next morning and never returned to Herod's palace.

That same night, an angel warned Joseph about Herod and told him to get up quickly, to take Mary and Jesus and to leave for Egypt immediately. This they did.

Herod waited and waited for the three kings to return. Finally his fortune-tellers told him that he had been tricked. The Magi were already on their way back home. Herod became so angry he turned red and then purple. His eyes bulged with hate.

"I will not be mocked by a mere baby. If I don't know which one to kill, I will kill them *all*. I will be free of this bothersome worry and be King forever!" He clenched his fists and screamed for his soldiers.

He ordered them to kill every boy two years old and younger in Bethlehem. Again, he thought up a clever trick and a cruel one. He knew if the mothers knew what he was up to, they would run in all directions trying to hide their children, and the soldiers couldn't go every which way at once. One would be bound to escape and it could be the Infant King.

So Herod invited the mothers to gather in the public square for a party to celebrate the birth of his own new son. Everyone was excited, for a party meant a chance to exchange stories of their children and wear their best clothes and eat a cake baked by someone else. So they bathed their sons and brushed their hair and told them to mind their manners.

It was a terrible moment when Herod's soldiers came and took their children from them and carried out the King's orders. If you, right now, can feel sadness in reading this, can you imagine how much more sorrow filled the hearts of those mothers?

Bethlehem was now a town with only little girls. There were no sounds of little boys chasing each other in and out of each other's houses, or making roads with their toy trucks, or playing ball with their fathers after supper.

The only thought that gave comfort to the young mothers was that one child did escape, the one whom Herod feared. For all his wise men and fortune-tellers and soldiers, Herod had no power to compare with that of angels' warnings and God's will.

The Holy Innocents were the first martyrs, the "flower buds nipped by frost" for Christ's sake. These little ones did not die for Christ because they knew what they were doing. They died because they were there and *could* have been Christ. They died, but our Lord lived, and because he lived, none of us shall ever die.

The next time your two-year-old brother scribbles with red crayon on your homework, or dumps his orange juice *again,* don't swat him or yell for your mother to *do* something with him. Just remember that he is an *Innocent* whom God gave to your family as a special gift. And put away your crayons.

Nicholas

December 6

nce upon a time in the country of Lycia, there lived a saint called Nicholas who is said to have worked a miracle the day he was born. As his nurse was giving him his first bath, he stood up straight, clasped his hands and looked up to heaven. Now, it takes some months before a baby can crawl or hold onto something, much less stand right up. So when Nicholas did this, everyone there knew that this was a very special baby.

He grew up as a happy child in a loving and comfortable family. They had more than enough of everything; perhaps that is why Nicholas never thought about money, or about holding on to it. He shared his marbles and graham crackers as easily as breathing, and if a friend said, "My, that's a good-looking shirt," he would take it right off and give it to him.

And once he gave something, he never stood around watching to make sure the person used it wisely. "Once you give a gift, let it go," he would say. "It is no longer yours, so go and tend to your own business."

When Nicholas was a young man, his parents died and left him a large fortune, and he made it his business to give it away. Not all at once in one big lump, but in his own way. Besides giving presents, Nicholas loved planning secret surprises. If he had been born at another time to other parents, he might have become an actor.

Instead, he used all his talents along with his wealth to live as a mysterious gift-giver. He would ride through town in the night, his cloak flying in the wind, a silk mask over his eyes, throwing a little bag of gold pieces through a window or doorway, or leaving it in the milk bottle on the porch, and then ride back off into the dark.

For years he did this, seeking out those who had the most need—a father who needed money to marry off his daughters, a farmer who needed a new ox, a widow who needed oatmeal and raisins for her children. He would see to it that they got the gold to take care of their needs. And he gave presents to children that weren't really needed but which made their eyes crinkle with joy and their feet jump up and down—almonds and oranges and silk scarves and calico kittens with blue eyes and Tootsie Rolls. Wouldn't he have made the nicest uncle who would come visiting with pockets crammed with such things?

We know that Nicholas must have been found out, for on his feast day, it is the custom in many countries to put your shoes outside your door the night before, and by morning St. Nicholas will have filled them with goodies. We carry on the custom by hanging up our Christmas stockings the night before our Lord is born, "in the hopes that St. Nicholas soon will be there." And he is bound to be there, for anyone who loves children and gifts and surprises as much as Nicholas would never miss *this* birthday!

When all Nicholas' money had been given away, Nicholas said, "Now I can become a priest and give away *more* than money." The first thing he did once he was a priest was to make a pilgrimage to the Holy Land, and he had to do this by boat. On the second day out, when Nicholas was still trying not to be seasick, a ferocious storm grabbed the boat and tossed it about the waves like an empty cracker box.

The old captain, who had weathered many storms, had never seen such a tempest as this. He and the crew grabbed onto anything fastened down and held on for dear life. Nicholas knelt down on the tilting deck, raised his eyes to heaven and prayed that they be saved. "I've only just begun, Lord, I have so much more to do!"

The captain yelled above the roar of the wind, "What good

are prayers now? Don't waste your breath! I'm going to tie you to the mast before you're swept over—''

Just then, the waves stopped churning, the black sky lightened and the sun began to shine so brightly it made rainbows in drops of water everywhere. Nicholas said, "You see, nothing is ever past praying for!"

And from that time, Nicholas has been the friend of sailors. Sometimes in the wildest of storms, sailors swear that they have seen him kneeling on the deck, with his arms outstretched as if to protect them.

Nicholas was such a good priest he soon became a bishop. His first love, after God, was for children. He would seek them out as he traveled the land to help them, protect them and sometimes even rescue them. Once in a town near his home, three little boys wandered off and got lost. They kept walking and soon came to a neat, pleasant-looking inn. It was painted gray and had red shutters and a sign over the gate that read: Dew Drop Inn. So they said, "Let's!" And they did.

The innkeeper listened to their story of being lost and said of course he would be *glad* to put them up for the night. He rubbed his hands together and smiled so hard you couldn't see his eyes. The boys were happy that they had found such a nice, understanding person but, as you will see, he was not really nice.

He was the kind of person who could look at three little boys and think how good they would be served up roasted, on a platter, with three bright red apples in their mouths. Or better yet, chopped up, put into a salty brine and pickled like pigs' feet.

Would you believe that this wicked man put his thoughts into action? By the next morning, the little boys were on their way to becoming pickles.

That very night, Nicholas had a nightmare which made him sit up in bed and count the thumpbeats of his heart. He had dreamed that three little boys had been chopped up and put into a tub of salty brine at the very inn he passed on his way to church.

In the morning, he dressed quickly and went straight to the

inn. The innkeeper was taken by surprise for it wasn't even seven o'clock yet. But he smiled and rubbed his hands greedily. Bishops were rich, he had heard, and people said this one was always giving away money, so he'd better be extra nice.

"Ah, Your Eminence," he bowed low, "Your Royal Churchly Excellency, what can this humble inn possibly offer you in keeping with your absolutely, perfectly presumptuous holy person? Ham and eggs? Sausage and pancakes? Cream of wheat?"

"How about," said Nicholas slowly, "some pickled pigs' feet? I woke this morning with an overwhelming craving you wouldn't believe. Isn't that some over there?" And he pointed to the old wooden tub with the boys in the brine.

The inkeeper grew very pale. "Oh no, Sir, Your Most Admirable Royalness, that's not ready yet."

"Why not?" asked Nicholas, rising slowly and towering over the quaking man. "Is it because it is too fresh? Is it because there are no pigs' feet in there, only three little boys chopped up?"

The innkeeper fell to his knees, shaking and wailing. He had been found out. What would happen to him? Nicholas went to the tub, raised his eyes to heaven and made the Sign of the Cross over the bits and pieces buried under the brine.

The water bubbled a little, as if something were stirring around at the bottom, and then up popped three very wet little heads. They smiled at the bishop and all three said in one voice: "What a marvelous sleep I've had!"

The innkeeper fainted from the shock. When he came to, he knelt down with Nicholas and the boys and prayed for forgiveness. From that day on, the innkeeper never again gave customers the wrong change, or stole money from the pockets of sleeping guests, or served pickled pigs' feet unless they were just that.

Lucy

December 13

ot too long after Jesus' time, in the country of Sicily there lived a bright little girl named Lucy. Her name comes from the Latin word *lux*, which means light, and she was indeed one of the brightest lights of the early Church.

She spent a happy childhood as the apple of everyone's eye, especially her parents'. When her father died, her life changed, but her sunny manner did not. True to her name, she tried to look on the bright side of things. She helped cheer her mother who had become sad and sickly now that her husband was gone.

She would fluff her mother's pillows and brush her hair as she talked. "Mother, you know Daddy is in heaven, so why do you cry? We'll be there with him someday. We just have to be patient." They knew death was not the end of everything because they were Christians, and Christians were often close to death, for it was a crime in those days to follow Christ.

Her mother agreed and tried to think happy thoughts, but she seemed to grow worse. Soon she could not even walk. She had to be carried about or pushed around in a wheelchair. Lucy had a dream in which St. Agatha told her to go to her tomb 50 miles away to pray for a cure for her mother. Lucy told her mother, and they both felt it would be good for them to get out of the house and make the trip. Maybe, just maybe, if it were God's will, her mother would soon be well.

After three days of walking and pushing the wheelchair up and down hills, they reached St. Agatha's tomb. It was quite late and they quickly fell asleep. Again, the saint appeared to Lucy in a dream and this time told her that her mother would be healed.

When Lucy woke the next day, sure enough it had happened! Her mother was already up. She stretched, braided her own hair, and declared she hadn't felt better in years. She left the wheelchair for someone who might need it and walked home so briskly Lucy had a hard time keeping up with her.

Lucy had been thinking about something very important since her father died and decided to tell her mother about it now. "I want to give the money Father gave me to all the people who have less than we do, Mother. I want to be poor as Jesus was. And another thing. I really don't want to marry the nice young man you chose for me. He is well-off, I know, but he will never believe as we do. Besides, I want to follow Jesus and no other man."

Her mother was so happy and grateful to Lucy for taking her to be cured that she would grant her anything. "You may do as you wish, Lucy dear, but I do hope your fiance won't be too upset."

But he *was* very upset, and not at all as nice as Lucy had thought. "If I can't have Lucy, then no one shall," he snarled spitefully, and he went to the Governor to turn her in.

"Lucy is a Christian and worships a strange God instead of our Roman ones," he told him. The Governor ordered that Lucy must be killed in the manner of the day. That meant she would be tied to the horns of two mean-tempered bulls and dragged through the streets as a warning to other Christians.

So they bound Lucy's hands and ankles tight and tied two leather ropes around her waist. The other ends of the ropes were tied to the bulls' horns. The soldiers cracked their whips across the bulls' backs and the angry beasts charged down the street, snorting and tossing their heads. But Lucy remained on her spot as if rooted in cement. The leather ropes snapped and the bulls raced off to nowhere in clouds of dust.

The soldiers tried again, this time with two wild-eyed stallions, and the same thing happened. The crowd was muttering. They had come to see a young Christian put to death, and here she stood, hands and feet bound, gazing off into the sky and humming to herself. They pushed her and tore at her robe and stepped on her toes, but still they could not budge her from the spot.

"Enough of this," growled the Governor, who was greatly irritated by this stubborn girl. He ran into the street, drew out his sword, and plunged it into Lucy's throat. She went to heaven immediately, where Jesus was waiting to welcome her and show her about her new home.

To this day, Lucy doesn't forget those who need her on earth. All over the world people with sore eyes pray for her to send down her "lucy-light" to help them see better, and anyone with a sore throat would, as you can imagine, find her very sympathetic.

In Sweden she is the patron of schoolgirls. On her feast day, little girls in Sweden and Norway wear a crown of candles and flowers in their hair and, as a special treat, bring their mothers breakfast in bed.

If you lived in Hungary, you would plant a few grains of wheat on Lucy's feast day so that you would have a pot of new green sprouts by Christmas. This is to remind us that we never ever die. Like the winter wheat and Lucy, when we seem to "die," we are really reborn into another life, as full of untold delight as God has promised.

John the Evangelist

nce upon a time there was an apostle named John who was so much like Jesus even Mary thought of him as a second son. John, who was a fisherman, became Jesus' disciple at the age of 18 when he and his brother James were sitting by the sea mending their nets.

Jesus came along, followed by Peter and then Andrew. He looked into James' and John's eyes and said, "Come, follow me." So they picked up their nets, joined the line and followed him.

Our Lord loved each of his apostles equally with a deep personal love. He knew their faults and how they would fail him—for they were human as we all are—but that did not lessen his love one bit.

But of all of them, it was John he called his "Beloved Disciple." John was always there when Jesus needed him. It was John and Peter who prepared the Last Supper. It was John who laid his head on Jesus' chest out of love and sorrow when our Lord said that one of them would betray him.

John was the only one of the 12 apostles to be at the foot of the Cross when Jesus hung from it. It was he who put his strong young arm around Mary to give her the comfort of knowing she was not alone. Jesus looked down upon them and gasped so low they could barely hear, "Woman, behold your son. Son, behold your mother." He gave John the special job of taking care of Mary for the rest of her life, and from that

moment, Mary and John were as mother and son.

　　After Mary died and her body and soul went straight up to heaven, John knew that it was time for him to go on to other work. At Pentecost, the Holy Spirit had stirred up the apostles to put on their sandals and go forth to spread God's good news.

　　They scattered to all parts of the world. John went to Ephesus to teach the Greek and Roman pagans all about what they called the *Logos* (the Word). He was so successful that the Emperor Domitian, who hated Christians, sent soldiers to bring him back to Rome to be thrown into a huge black pot of boiling oil.

　　John was ready to leave this world as a martyr, even though

he didn't feel he had done all he could, but to his surprise and the Emperor's anger, John stepped out of the pot unhurt and unscalded, with his skin as pink and fresh as a wild rose.

The Emperor did not want to throw him back into the pot for fear the miracle would happen again. So he banished John to the island of Patmos. When Domitian died, John came back to Ephesus, and here he accomplished his second special job: He wrote the fourth Gospel of the New Testament.

Matthew, Mark and Luke had already written their accounts of Christ's life, and now John added his. Mark began his Gospel with Jesus' public life. Matthew and Luke started with his birth. But John went clear back to the very beginning.

Before the world was made, he said, and long before he was born as Mary's baby, Jesus was God's Son or Word. For the beginning of his Gospel, John wrote a beautiful poem about Jesus coming to bring God's eternal light into the world, and it is read in church on Christmas Day.

All of John's writing tried to open our eyes and hearts to God's love for us. He urges us:

• "Let us not love one another merely with words, but in deed and in truth!"

• "If you do not love your brother whom you can see, how can you love God whom you cannot see?"

• "He who has love has the life of God in him. God is love!"

And over and over he says, "My children, love one another." When people asked him why he said the same thing so many times, he answered, "Because it is the Word of the Lord, and if you keep it, you do enough."

Saints Budding Everywhere

Winter/Spring

In January, all is death. The green of grass and trees and hope is gone. The sun itself is bored and retires before supper. The garden, lush with the overflow of tomatoes and squash in fall, lies stark and stricken by the plague of frost. Blackened vines crunch underfoot, and the mole starts tunneling his winter home across the lawn. The wind whistles through abandoned cornstalks and whines around the limbs of the apple tree.

The last remnants of summer, brown leaves and wizened fruit, lie hidden on the ground; the snow silently covers all. The garden is dead, left to the scavenger crew of crows.

But we know better! The bear sleeps in his cave and the squirrels set up house in our attic. The sap is churning in the grapevines and the maples; and strawberries and rhubarb and asparagus are waiting to push through the April snow. What seems dead is only hidden.

So too the hardy perennial of our faith grows quietly in the winter of the soul. We are rooted in the most extraordinary, magnificent Vine which no drought, fire or ice can kill, no root can wither, no snake can crush. And its branches—an intricate, varied arbor—go their way, wandering, climbing, twisting, dancing, crawling under fences, spiraling around steeples. With the Vine as our home base, so do we make our way like a prayer to the Sun.

The saints in this section have carried the reach of the Vine beyond the sight of their Italian or German or Japanese gardens. They were like dandelion seeds, blown to every corner of creation by a puff from God. They buried themselves in winter soil and were reborn like spring flowers in God's. They grew in their own corners of his garden, in their own way. They all abided in the Vine, and the Vine in them; and they bore much fruit to the glory of God.

Elizabeth Seton

January 4

here was once a little girl who became a saint by *looking up*. She didn't spend her life flying kites, or plastering ceilings, or searching the sky for geese in spring. Her *looking-up* was a bigger, grander thing. It was a great umbrella which covered every happening of her life.

Her name was Elizabeth Ann Bayley, and she was born into a wealthy Episcopalian family in New York City in 1774. It was an exciting time to come into the world, for our country itself would be born in two years and New York City would be its first capital. Hearts were filled with hope and quick to promise the hard work needed for true independence.

Elizabeth's story, as the years went by, was like that of the American pioneers who were stalwart in hardship, ever pressing on to their goal. But her goal was not to reach an outpost in the northern wilds or a settlement in the desert. It was to do God's will wherever he put her.

She didn't think of such things as she grew up amid the comforts and pleasures enjoyed by well-to-do young ladies in New York society. Elizabeth was properly proficient in French and music and good manners. She went to the theater and read the latest novels and went shopping for ball gowns and Swiss chocolates. She dutifully read her daily Scripture and went to Trinity Episcopal Church on Sunday, but she wasn't extraordinarily pious. Every now and then she would dramatically announce that she wanted to join the Quakers. And when shocked friends would ask why on earth *why,* she would laugh, "Because they have such pretty little bonnets!"

When she went to parties, all the young men had their eyes on the charming Miss Bayley with the merry brown eyes. But these brown eyes could see only one man. His name was William Magee Seton. His family owned a shipping firm and was also wealthy. Both families were delighted at the thought of such a match. Such a handsome pair—they were made for each other!

Elizabeth and William felt they were too, so at the age of 19 she became Mrs. William Seton. They began their life together in a mansion, one of the many which lined Wall Street in New York City, and William joined his father in the business. Life was heavenly and Elizabeth dreamed that all their life would be sweet. They would raise a family, she and Will, and go to church on Sunday. And she would do charity work on Thursday and have a Literary Tea on Monday. And in the evening, when the children were in bed, she would sew or read while Will played his Stradivarius violin, which he would make sing with his touch. Her world was perfect, and she had no wish to change it. But God did.

It began when her father-in-law died and Will had to take over the business. It did not go well. Ships were lost to storms at sea or were taken by pirates. Will would fret and worry as the fortune slipped away. Elizabeth took care of the books and tried to pay the bills, but try as they might to keep it going, the business failed.

The young couple felt the first pinch of hardship. They moved to a smaller house and began selling furniture to buy food for the family. Creditors banged on the door, demanding their payment. Will was depressed and could not find work. Elizabeth would try to cheer him and he would hug her tightly, calling her his "old knot of oak."

He began to cough and grow thinner and weaker each day. What Elizabeth feared was true: He had tuberculosis and needed much rest. Her father, who was a doctor, worried that she and the children (by now there were five) would also catch some disease in the crowded city, so the family spent the summer with Dr. Bayley on Long Island.

At that time, Dr. Bayley was the health officer for the city of New York. His work was to examine the newly-arrived immigrants from Ireland. Elizabeth went with him to help, and her heart was saddened by the condition of the newcomers. She had never seen such sickness and hunger and pinched, gaunt cheeks. But she saw no despair. The name of God was on the immigrants' tongues and rosaries rubbed to a shine were wound around the hands of young and old. How strong was the faith of these immigrants!

They were coming into a land of opportunity—and disease. The dreaded yellow fever was an epidemic in New York. Dr. Bayley had tried in vain to clean up the stagnant swamps around the city and the mounds of garbage where the germs bred. But by the end of that summer, he too caught the fever and died.

Elizabeth was numb with grief. Then her husband took a turn for the worse. The young wife remembered the Psalms she had read in her childhood. Bit by bit they came back to her and put her heart at peace. "I have become a *looker-up*," she told her children. "We shall not worry. God will get us through and Daddy will get better and we shall be a family as we used to be once again."

A sea journey was what Will needed, she decided. The fresh salty air, the clear sky, rest—that would do it. So she sold the house and her family possessions—the silver, the crystal, even the gold locket with her mother's picture. The one thing she could not bear to sell was Will's violin, which she gave to a friend for safekeeping. Anna, the oldest, went with them, but William, Richard, Catherine and Rebecca, who were too young, stayed at home.

Will coughed less and seemed stronger during the voyage. When they saw the green hills of Italy coming into view, their spirits were high. Will was getting better and they would be staying with the Setons' good friends, the Filicchi family. Antonio Filicchi was waiting at the dock, waving, and they hurried to leave the ship and join him. Suddenly a sailor blocked their way and refused to let them off. They were to be kept in quarantine until it was certain they had not brought in any yellow fever germs from New York.

For 40 days they were kept on an island in a stone, prison-like building called the Lazaretto. Elizabeth remembered the immigrants from Ireland for whom she had felt such pity. Now she knew how they had felt. The Setons' room had nothing: no heat, bed, chairs, food—nothing. A mattress was brought in for Will. The wind from the sea whistled and whined through a crack in the wall. Elizabeth looked up and asked, "Lord, please do something!"

Antonio showed up the next day, as welcome as a guardian angel. He brought blankets, food, wood, some wine—even curtains and some toys for Anna and a servant, Luigi. Luigi ran errands, brought medicine, tended the fire. Will no longer seemed to be improving, but Elizabeth hid her fears from Anna. Together they played games and jumped rope to keep warm.

When they were finally allowed to leave two weeks before Christmas, Will was a shivering bag of bones, sicker than ever. The Filicchis took the tenderest care of their friend, but it was too late. Two days after Christmas, Will's tired heart stopped beating and he died. Elizabeth was now a widow.

The Filicchis tried to cheer her with trips to the city to visit art museums and churches. When they invited her to go to Mass with them she accepted, curious about this religion that seemed as important to her wealthy Italian friends as it was to the poor Irish immigrants. When she knelt before the Blessed Sacrament, she was filled with a peace she had not known before. She felt a turning inside her, a giving over of her soul which she called "an entire surrender of itself and all its faculties to God."

Despite the kindness of the Filicchi family and the new spiritual questioning within her heart, Elizabeth was at a crossroads and knew that she must return home to find her way. Here she sat, a young widow, penniless in a foreign country. What would she do? Where would she go? Why had God allowed this to happen?

Deep in her soul, she knew there was a reason. She had

enough faith, even then, to look up and to trust that out of the worst comes the best. "Afflictions," she later wrote, "are the steps to heaven. Have confidence! Never let the comparison of time and eternity slip an instant from your mind. I find this cures all sorrow."

Elizabeth decided to leave Italy and get on with a life for herself and her children. How she missed them! As she and Anna boarded the ship to America, Antonio hugged her and said, "Never fear, my child. God, who takes care of the birds and lilies, will take care of you, too!"

Four healthy and happy children awaited them in New York. The first thing Elizabeth did was find a small apartment in the house of a friend. Then she decided to open a school for girls in her home. Parents were only too happy to send students to lovely Mrs. Seton who had known such tragedy. She was soon making a fair living and was even able to buy some treats for the children and books for herself.

Elizabeth began to think more and more about the Catholic faith. She went to her minister at Trinity Church for advice. He was very shocked and not at all sympathetic. In fact, he was quite angry.

"I told you those Catholics in Italy would poison your mind! You must stay away from them and their religion. I tell you, if you become a Catholic I will have nothing more to do with you!"

So Elizabeth did nothing for a year but pray and wonder and worry. A letter from Antonio urged her to study both religions to find the truth for herself. "Whatever you do," he wrote, "I am your friend forever." So she studied and, finally, one day in March, 1804, she walked into St. Peter's church on Barclay Street and told the priest, "I want to become a Catholic."

These words changed Elizabeth's life. Her relatives, except for her sisters-in-law Cecilia and Harriet (who would one day follow her into the Church), would have nothing more to do with her or her children. "How could any intelligent, well-bred woman make such a mistake? And those poor little children, she'll probably make Catholics out of them, too!" Elizabeth Seton was a good topic of gossip at many afternoon teas.

Parents immediately took their children out of her school and she soon was running out of money. She gathered her children around her and hugged them. "Well, my loves, it seems we are off on another adventure. Never mind. Don't sniffle, Rebecca. God is with us, so what shall we fear? We won't look behind or before, only *up*."

Where would they go? The Filicchis had invited them to come to Italy, but Elizabeth felt she should stay in America since it was her home. Then she received a letter from a priest in Baltimore, Maryland, asking if she would come there since they were very much in need of Catholic teachers. He would also provide a home for her at the school.

Baltimore! It was so far from New York, from all she knew. But Elizabeth trusted in God's direction. She would go with complete, accepting enthusiasm. She wrote, "I am gently, quietly, silently a Catholic; the difficulties are all past; only a few knotty ones there are who must talk of something, and the worst they say is: 'So much trouble has turned her brain.'. . . At all events, happen now what will, I rest in God."

On a sunny June morning Elizabeth set sail down the coast to Baltimore with her three daughters (the boys were away at boarding school) and Harriet and Cecilia. They were welcomed by the priest on their arrival and given a red brick house—"a neat, delightful mansion with folding windows"—where they would live and teach school. Here they lived for a year while Elizabeth wrestled with another question. She wanted to become a nun. But how could she, with three young daughters still living with her?

Bishop John Carroll, who had confirmed her in New York, gave her permission not only to become a nun, but also to start a new community similar to the one founded by St. Vincent de Paul in France. It would be called the Sisters of Charity.

And so Elizabeth (now called Mother Seton), her new community of seven sisters plus her three daughters left Baltimore for their new home 50 miles away in Emmitsburg. They set off in a covered wagon piled high with mattresses, chairs, pots and pans, lanterns, candles, soaps, linens and, packed very carefully on top, Will's violin, with which Elizabeth would never part.

The wagon bumped and jogged along for three days until they reached their log-cabin home on the side of the mountain. Here they lived until their new home was built. The sisters met the adventure with high spirits. Elizabeth writes of walking to the mountain church: "There was no bridge over the creek. . .and when the water was high, we had to cross one by one on horseback; when it was low, we passed over the stones. . . ." Sometimes Elizabeth would sit on "her" rock and teach catechism to the children of the parish.

The first winter in their new home, which they called the Stone House, was a hard one. The snow often sifted down on the sisters through the roof as they slept. Food was in short supply and they survived on what Providence sent. Sometimes it wasn't what they felt like eating, but Elizabeth, with her way of stirring up fun, made light of the scanty cupboards. If someone gave them a bushel of turnips, she would pretend she had to make a serious decision.

"Now what shall we have for supper tonight? Cream of turnip soup with a dash of nutmeg? Followed by mashed turnip cakes with caraway seed? Followed by a dessert of turnip and dried apple pudding and carrot-top coffee?"

The sisters would groan and Elizabeth would laugh. "Cheer up, it could be a bushel of horseradish. Or sauerkraut!"

Spring came, and the sisters planted a garden and bought chickens and pigs and a cow. Their spirits thrived and so did their school, which Elizabeth called St. Joseph's Free School. Both black and white children attended and, since most were poor, Elizabeth made sure they had snacks of apples and cookies and milk each day.

That stone house was the first Catholic parochial school in the United States. Soon so many pupils came that the sisters had to build a larger school and then a convent to train novices so they might go out to other cities and teach. The Bishop of Philadelphia asked her to send nuns to open the first Catholic orphanage there, and three nuns were requested for the same purpose in New York City. All this happened within two years after Elizabeth sailed out of New York City.

Her personal life was filled with comings and goings of a

sadder sort. Her son Richard was lost at sea. Her devoted sisters-in-law, Harriet and Cecilia, died within a few months of each other. They were followed a few years later in death by her daughters Anna and Rebecca. All were buried by a large oak in the cemetery at St. Joseph's School. Elizabeth, who died at the age of 46, lies near them, buried within the chapel close by.

In her short life Elizabeth Seton was Episcopalian society belle, wife, mother, teacher and Catholic nun. She never lost sight of her goal: to do God's will. And she never tired of *looking up*.

John Neumann

January 5

his is the story of a little man who had a gigantic dream. He was not especially handsome or charming; he had no important friends or family, little money or encouragement. Everything about him was ordinary. He looked like the man who sells mousetraps in the back of the hardware store or who mops the floor of the market at closing time—the kind of man you look at but don't see. Yet, by God's grace, he became the bishop of the city of Philadelphia.

This good, plain man, God's little acorn, was John Neumann. He was born in Bohemia (now part of Czechoslovakia) in 1811. He was a good child who neither caused trouble nor raised high expectations. No one was surprised when he entered the seminary to become a good, plain priest. He studied and studied and found he had a way with words and languages. By the time he was ready to become a priest, he could speak French, German, English and Italian, as well as Latin and Greek. In later years, when he was in America, he would add Gaelic to the list.

John was very short. Even when he was full-grown, he barely reached five feet, two inches. As for the rest of him, he had a broad face and the large, work-worn hands of a farmer. His manner was pleasant and quiet, but underneath this surface was the determination to make real the dream God had given him: to travel to America and minister to the German immigrants. Many people were leaving Germany for America, and John sympathized with these uprooted plants trying to put down new roots in a strange land. They needed the comfort and caring of a spiritual advisor with whom they could talk in their mother tongue, he felt, someone with whom to share old memories and new problems.

He waited eagerly for his ordination day. To his disappointment it had to be delayed because the bishop was ill. So he decided he would go to America and be ordained there. Why waste time?

Thus on a winter's day, he said good-bye to his family, trying not to think that he probably would not see them again. He hugged his mother one more time, wiped away his tears and climbed aboard the stagecoach.

After a rough, joggling trip of 50 days, he arrived in Paris with $40 in his pocket. Here he lived as his money slowly melted away, waiting for answers to his applications to serve in the United States. For months he waited with no response. Finally one day in 1835, an envelope stamped *New York* arrived and John was overjoyed. He had been accepted as an assistant in a parish in Buffalo!

Within the week he set sail on a three-masted schooner bound for New York with only the clothes on his back and one last dollar in his pocket. Forty days later he arrived in a very shabby condition. His clothes had not been changed since the beginning of the trip! But John had no concern about his appearance or other people's opinion of him. When he was finally ordained in Albany in 1836, how he looked on the outside had not the slightest connection with the happiness that was in his heart. He felt as if he were wearing royal purple velvet, for he was a priest at last.

John made his way to Buffalo along the Erie Canal by boat and train. He was impatient to begin his work! But when he arrived, he found a different picture than his hopes had painted. His church was a half-built building without roof or windows. There was no rectory, no school, no welcoming committee. His home was an attic room in an inn with no closet. "Well," he chuckled, "I have no use for one anyhow."

He soon found that the people of the area had little use for Catholics. They threw mud and manure over the walls of the roofless church; often they found their mark as he said Mass.

John realized that the immigrants living in this unfriendly place had even more need of him, so he thanked God for sending him here. He never missed a day of visiting, even during the fierce and bitter Buffalo winters when icy, howling winds chased at his heels as he made his way from house to house. He served not only German families, but Irish, French and Italian as well.

They, in turn, took care of their "little father" and knitted him caps and sweaters to warm him against the cold. But he would pass on the clothing to those who, he felt, needed it more. The women would then scold him for being indifferent to their hours of hard work. "How do you think I like to see the beautiful red cap I knitted for Father on the head of lazy old Fritz who drinks?" muttered one. And John would gently remind her what Christ said about clothing the naked and having two coats in your closet. She would understand, but she would still mutter.

After a few years in Buffalo, John decided that he wanted to belong to a community of priests, so he asked permission to join the Redemptorist order. He became a novice in their seminary in Pittsburgh, where there was a need for German-speaking priests. He was sent to work in New York and Ohio and Virginia, and he went willingly. He wanted to touch as many lives as possible.

John did his work so well he was called back to Pittsburgh and told that he had been chosen to be the new general superior of all the Redemptorists in America. This meant he would be in charge of schools, parishes, convents—everything the Redemptorists did—and of getting the money to run them.

This was not for John! To be superior of men older than himself, to be a businessman, or in charge of running anything—oh no, this was not why he had come to America! He wanted only the hard, simple life of a parish priest.

Then he remembered the day in Paris when he opened that

envelope and knew his prayer had been answered. He had vowed that he would be God's man always, doing what God willed. It would seem that now, by God's will and grace, he was to be the new general superior. Very well, then, he would get to work.

And he did. He did his work so well God gave him an even harder job. A bishop was needed in the diocese of Philadelphia, and John was nominated. He was shocked. He was speechless. He went quickly to the bishop who would be leaving and, on his knees and in tears, pleaded not to be considered.

"Can't you tell I'm not right for this job?" he begged. "Look at me! Do I *look* like a bishop? Do I *sound* like a bishop? How many bishops do you know with just one pair of shoes?" His pleas made no difference.

John asked the nuns in the convents, schoolchildren, families in the parishes—everyone—to pray for his special intention (which was, *"Please-God-don't-let-me-be-a-bishop!")*. He even wrote to his superior in Rome, asking him to tell the pope that John was not right for the job.

But nothing worked. God would have his way with John. So he sighed, and accepted. "I *guess* You know best. I had better get to work."

In the remaining nine years of his life, John worked to build more schools and parishes. He founded a teaching order of nuns and brought other orders, such as the Christian Brothers, into the city. And he wrote a German-American catechism in his spare time.

At first people would look at John and think, *"He* is our bishop?"—just as John knew they would. A visiting archbishop once wrote back in a report to Rome that John was "a little inferior, for the importance of such a distinguished city as Philadelphia, rich, intelligent, full of life and importance, surely merits a bishop of another type. . . ." (You'd think an archbishop would know better than to judge such a holy book by its cover and size.)

And when he died at the age of 49, a pious old lady who came by to pay her last respects commented, "Why, to see that humble creature, you'd never think he was a bishop!"

John, standing tall in heaven, might have replied, "Exactly right, dear lady. I am proof that God can do anything. He can even turn an acorn like me into an oak of a bishop. Isn't it amazing?"

Thomas Aquinas

January 28

nce upon a time there was a little boy named Thomas who asked questions all day long. When he woke he asked why the sun rose in the east, and when he got dressed he asked who invented shoelaces and soap, and when he ate breakfast he asked what raisins looked like before they were raisins and why biscuits rose in the oven and how chickens lay eggs. When his mother finally shooed him outside he asked the gardener why the grass was green, where spiders go in winter and when bees sleep. At night he wanted to know why the sun set in the west, where he went when he slept, and could he please have another glass of water?

But the question he asked most, day and night, was "What is God?"

Thomas' mother, Teodora, had 12 other children to take care of, and his prattle exasperated her thoroughly. He was always underfoot, and since he was a quite large little boy, it could be dangerous for her to be tripping over him constantly.

"Thomas," she would snap, "stop that jabbering and go out and pick off the potato bugs." Or, "Please go next door and borrow a cup of olive oil." Thomas, who was very mild-mannered and obedient, would do what she said. Then he would bounce right back, asking her, "What is God?" Teodora said he was just like a fly hovering about her head on a hot day.

70

But both Teodora and his father Landolfo knew that Thomas was a "different" child and that God must have a special purpose for him. They didn't know what. At first they thought he was slow-witted, because he didn't talk much or move quickly or get excited about anything. They could not possibly imagine the exciting life that was going on in his brain.

His family were wealthy and respected citizens of the town of Roccasecca. At that time, sons of wealthy nobleman became either knights or priests. Thomas certainly showed no talent for fighting, so his parents decided he would become a monk. At the age of five they sent him off to the nearby Benedictine abbey of Monte Cassino. Maybe the monks could answer his never-ending questions, they hoped.

Teodora and Landolfo also hoped that Thomas would become a learned monk, perhaps even the abbot of the monastery in time. Wouldn't they all be proud of him then! They already had soldiers and a poet in the family and, no doubt, a daughter or two would become nuns—but an abbot, that would be a real feather in their cap!

So off Thomas went to the abbey. He did so well that by the time he was 12 the monks could teach him no more; they sent him to the University of Naples for more study. Thomas loved the city and all the opportunities he had to learn.

One day he went into a Dominican church, knelt down and instantly felt a great peace. Something in his heart said, "This is it, Thomas. Here you will find your answers." And the friars welcomed him, little knowing what a very special soul God had directed to them.

After three more years Thomas, who was 20 now, asked the Dominicans if he could join them, and they were as joyful as he in accepting him. They already suspected that within this large body (he stood six feet, six inches tall, with a great square head set on a thick neck) was a mind the likes of which the world had not seen.

So with great pride he put on his rough black and white woolen habit and made ready to go to Rome to study. He was a bit worried about how his mother would take the news. He knew she and the family would be upset, but *upset* wasn't the word. They were *furious!*

In those days, the Dominicans and the Franciscans were not well thought of. They were considered strange, radical dreamers, with neither bed nor roof nor food to give them security.

"This is absolutely unheard of!" said his mother, white with anger. "I will not have my son looking like a beggar and acting like a beggar, going about in sandals and begging for crusts. Oh, what terrible shame has come to us!" Then she fainted and was taken to her room, where she stayed for three days. During that time she planned how she would save Thomas from such a fate.

She called on two of her soldier sons and told them to capture Thomas and bring him home until he came to his senses. So they did. They hid in the bushes along the road and as he walked by, counting the stars, they jumped out, knocked him to the ground and tied him with rope. At first it was quite a struggle because Thomas was very strong. But finally he gave in and held tight to his habit so it wouldn't get ripped in the scuffle.

His family took him to the tower of their castle and kept him prisoner there for a year. His younger sisters brought him books secretly, and he used the days and weeks learning the Scriptures backwards and forwards. Finally, a soft-hearted sister, Marotta (who became a nun much later), made plans with the Dominicans to help Thomas escape.

Somehow they sneaked a huge basket into his room and packed him into it and *somehow,* like Paul, he was pushed through the window and lowered safely to the ground. With the waiting Dominicans he quickly escaped off into the night. (When we get to heaven, I'd like to find out just how Thomas' sisters got him through that tiny tower window!)

He went to Paris and then to the university at Cologne, Germany, to study with one of the finest of the Dominican teachers, St. Albert the Great. Thomas said little but his brain never stopped listening and working. The other students considered him dull because he didn't enjoy arguing or showing off in class. They made fun of him behind his back and called him the Dumb Ox.

Albert just smiled because he knew that someday the joke would be on them. "You may call him a dumb ox," he shook his finger at them, "but some day you will hear his bellowing all over the world."

Soon after Thomas was ordained, he returned to Paris to study, teach, lecture and write about the Christian faith. Students were eager to be in his classes because he set their minds spinning. He did not believe in presenting answers to be learned. Instead, he led his pupils to think for themselves and to find their own answers.

And in all his writings (he wrote over 60 books), he led his readers to do the same thing—*think* for themselves. He didn't want people to accept the truths about God and his creations just because someone *told* them to. He said that nothing that was true or right could be proven wrong, so they should discuss and reason and use their intelligence. "It is holiness itself, using natural talents to witness to the truth," he said.

The most famous of his books is called the *Summa Theologica,* in which he explained and defended the Christian beliefs. Thomas could never stop asking questions—and then answering them. In this book he answered over 10,000 questions, or objections, which non-Christians had about our faith.

Even greater than his mind was a heart that was unable to love anything, even learning, more than God. The love he had for our Lord spilled over onto everyone he met and they, in turn, soaked up his gentle love like a blotter in the rain. He drew as many into the Church by his warm charm as by the cold brilliance of his mind. He enjoyed nature and art and music and said that "they who abhor pleasures are boorish and ungracious." And to be boorish and ungracious would be to be inconsiderate of others' feelings; our Lord certainly wouldn't want that!

He loved to touch things—pussy willows, cool marble, mud, a kitten's tongue—and said no one could be a good thinker unless he or she was a good toucher. And he had a well-developed funnybone that enjoyed playfulness; he called it a sin to be sour-faced and "burdensome to others, showing no amusement and acting as a wet blanket."

We know that he was fat—fat enough, it is said, that a hole had to be cut out of the table so he could fit in. We don't know why he was fat. It doesn't seem likely that a saint would steal downstairs at night and eat 10 peanut butter and jelly sandwiches for a snack. Since Thomas didn't talk about it, we don't know if his large size bothered him. It certainly must have been uncomfortable at times. But Thomas may have been absent-minded enough not to notice. He was so busy writing, he probably never bothered to look sideways in a mirror.

One day Thomas stopped writing after he had a vision during Mass. He laid his pen down and said, "I cannot go on. After all I have seen and all that has been revealed to me, all that I have written seems to me like so much rubbish."

He still traveled about teaching, lecturing and writing hymns which we still sing today at Benediction, but he knew that his work in this life was almost done. He was on his way to talk to a council in France when he fell ill. His secretary Reginald, who went with him everywhere, was able to help him reach a Benedictine monastery at Fossanuova, and Thomas agreed to stop for a little rest.

The monks were besides themselves with joy that they would be able to care for the great Thomas, who was no longer called the Dumb Ox. They hurried back and forth from the woods carrying armfuls of wood for the fire in his room. The warmth felt good to him, but in his kind way he begged them to stop. They might catch cold going out into those bitter winds.

The young secretary tried to cheer him up. "Can't I please get you something—some cream of asparagus soup, baked custard, *something?*"

Thomas thanked him and thought for a moment. He did remember something he especially liked from his years in Paris. "Ah, a bit of herring would taste so good. I haven't had it in years."

So Reginald ran around trying to find some herring, but to his dismay there were none to be found. A fishmonger passed by just then calling his wares. Reginald stopped him, "Please, sir, would you by some miracle have some herring? My master, Friar Thomas, is quite ill, and he would love a herring."

The fisherman frowned. "Got no herring, but how about a kipper? Kipper would make him chipper!"

"No, kipper won't do. Are you *sure* you have no herring?"

"Well, how about sardines? They taste pretty much like herring. Tell him they're baby herring."

So Reginald, feeling sad that he had failed, bought a basket of sardines. He brought it to Thomas, who opened the lid and sniffed with delight. "What a lovely basket of herring! And I thought I'd never taste them again. Such a nice treat—thank you, Reginald." And when Reginald peeked into the basket, he saw herring indeed—large, silvery, fat herring.

Thomas enjoyed a few bites of the fish and told Reginald to share all the rest with the monks. He knelt down slowly and prayed to the Lord for whom he had taught and written so many years. Thomas asked the Lord to forgive anything he did or said that might have been wrong.

And then he went to heaven, where he would finally find out for himself "What is God?"

Frances of Rome

March 9

nce upon a time, there was a housewife named Frances who felt her work was so important she kept God waiting until she finished it. If she had windows to wash, she'd ask him to please wait in the parlor while she polished every one. If it were Monday morning and she had laundry to hang out, she'd ask if he'd mind holding the clothespins while she hung it on the line. Even when she was kneeling deep in prayer, if the baby fell out of bed, she would stop her conversation with God and go to the child at once. "Sorry, Lord," she would say, "but you know how it is."

It wasn't that Frances thought so little of our Lord that she put everything else before him. It was because she believed in *first things first,* and what came first to her were her husband Lorenzo and her three children, Battista, Evangelist and Agnes. She knew that being a wife and mother to them was the way God wanted her to give her life for him, so she worked at making a home with as much devotion as a nun decorating the chapel for Easter.

You'd think this would have been easy for Frances; she had everything and everyone at hand to help her. She was both loving and lovable and very pretty besides, with dark brown eyes and dark brown hair piled atop her head like a fat, flat roll. Her husband and his family were wealthy and they all lived in a castle with balconies and gardens and turrets that reached to the sky. She had three cooks and a butler

77

and a gardener; upstairs maids and downstairs maids; and one maid who did nothing but brush her mistress' hair and polish her shoes.

But Frances had wanted none of this. What she had really wished with all her heart was to be a nun and spend her life serving only God. Her wealthy parents would have none of that. She would be doing God's will, they told her, only if she married the young nobleman, Lorenzo, and then everyone would be happy. So she did, and everyone—except Frances—was happy.

Oh, she wasn't *terribly* unhappy, because Lorenzo really did love his young bride (she was only 13) and so did his family. So Frances tucked away her sadness where only God could see it and said, "Very well, Lord, you want me to be a wife? Help me to be the best!"

She bustled about the castle and in a short time began to enjoy her role as mistress of the manor. She learned the first names of all 23 servants and investigated every nook and cranny of her new home. She pulled back the velvet drapes to let the sun shine in and made sure the linen sheets were ironed. She stocked the cellar with wood and wine and apples and the pantry shelves with garbanzo beans and plum jam and Lorenzo's rum tobacco. She was very busy putting *first things first*.

But sometimes, just now and then, when she was alone, she would remember how she had wanted to keep house for our Lord alone and keep *his* shelves stocked high with her good deeds. Then she would sit on a little stool in her closet and weep.

One day her sister-in-law Vannozza found her in such a mood and was quite upset. Whatever could be wrong with sunny Francesca who was never sad?

Frances loved Vannozza as if she were her real sister, so she wiped her eyes and confided in her. Vannozza burst out laughing. "You too, Francesca? I have wanted to be a nun all my life. Now here we are, brides together in this house! Come on, let's be brave and noble together and make this castle a happy place! Aren't we lucky we have each other?"

They vowed to serve God outside the castle as well, in whatever way they could. They asked their husbands if they might go out each day to help the poor of Rome, and their husbands gave them both money and blessings. Lorenzo kissed Frances as they went out the door with their hampers stuffed full of sausage and olive oil and garlic bread and parsley and tomatoes and little bouquets of marigolds and peppermint sprigs for the children.

"Go where God sends you, my dear," he smiled, "but be home for supper."

So the two young women began their new venture. They put on their plainest clothes and sweetest smiles and went out to make life easier for the needy in the busy city. In a few years, however, when Frances and Lorenzo were blessed with children, it was Vannozza who kept on the work with the poor. Frances stayed home and took care of the babies. She fed them and bathed them and rocked them to sleep and, in between that, she still managed the affairs of the castle.

"A woman such as I must never forget she is a housewife," she said to Vannozza, as they cut out molasses cookies. "Sometimes she must leave God at the altar and find him in her housekeeping." She put down her rolling pin and sighed, "Most of the time I feel like a yo-yo, pulled and spinning in every direction and getting absolutely nowhere." And Vannozza nodded her head, "How true!"

To our Lord, Frances apologized, "What do I have to give you? Just interruptions and distractions, bits and pieces of trying to do your will."

But our Lord understood about those interruptions and sent her a special gift to make her feel better. One morning Frances tiptoed out of bed to say her prayers. It was not yet dawn and a few sleepy stars were still winking. At last she had some time alone with our Lord! No sooner did she kneel down and open her book to morning prayers than Lorenzo called to her to come watch the sunrise. She marked her page and went at once to the window, and together they marveled at the purple sky turning pink, with a few puffs of whipped-cream clouds.

Very well. She had seen the sunrise, now back to her book. She knelt down and took out the marker—and there was a knock at the door. The downstairs maid popped in and bowed. There was a beggar at the kitchen door, would it be all right to give him the leftover liver and onions from the night before? "Of course," Frances said, "and give him the apple dumplings too."

She got back on her knees and opened the book to the same page. Another knock. This time it was the new young cook who couldn't remember whether to put the dill and garlic at the *bottom* of the jar or the top when she made the sour pickles. Frances told her the bottom, and praised her for being smart enough to ask.

The young girl hurried off and before Frances could close the door she heard little Agnes sobbing in the hallway. The boys had snatched her doll with the red hair and thrown it up into the plum tree. Frances hugged her and called to the gardener to rescue the doll. Then she found her sons and set them down to write *I must not tease my sister* 100 times. "And if you do it again," she warned them, "you will go to the cellar and crack one bushel of black walnuts."

Wearily, she closed the door—and then jumped a little with surprise. A magnificent angel bathed in light was writing something in her prayerbook. She came up quietly behind him and peeked over his shoulder. There, in a beautiful gold script, he had written: "Therefore, God has blessed you forever."

These were the very words where Frances had left off each time she had been interrupted. Frances looked at the angel with disbelief. "Why would God bless me when I can't sit still long enough to pray to him?"

"Because you showed your love for him by doing exactly what he wants you to do—loving and taking care of your family."

From that time on for the rest of her days on earth, Frances and her guardian angel were the best of friends. He came to her, it is said, in the form of a little golden-haired boy whom no one else but Frances could see. They visited and walked in the gardens and had tea. He even brought his own cup, which was invisible too.

Then a great plague swept across Italy and soon the streets of Rome were filled with the dying. Frances' happy world grew sad as first Evangelist and then Agnes died. A war broke out and Lorenzo and

Battista were carried off as prisoners. Frances and Vannozza ran out of food and money, so they sold their furs and jewels and silver candlesticks and crystal goblets. When the money from that was gone, they went door to door, begging for food and medicine to help the sick.

Frances thought her family life had come to an end. She was now alone. So she asked the bishop for permission to found an order of women who lived in the world, who made no vows but simply offered themselves to God to serve the poor. And she received it.

Then, out of the blue and to her joy, Lorenzo and Battista were set free and came home. She told Lorenzo about the society she wanted to form and call the Oblates of Mary and asked if he'd mind if she did that and still lived at the castle. "Of course not, my dear," he smiled, "as long as you are home for supper."

For three years Frances lived at home and worked with her Sisters during the day. Then Lorenzo died and Battista married; so Frances left her home of 40 years and went to live with the women of her community. She was so grateful to God that she was able to serve him now as she had wanted since she was a child.

One night when she was visiting Battista and his bride Mobilia, she felt tired. So she said her prayers and went to bed early. She felt a warmth on her face and opened her eyes. The room shone with a golden light, the color of the twilight sun on a winter afternoon.

She sat up and called to her son and his wife, "Goodbye, my loves! My angel has finished his task and holds my hand. I must follow!"

And so she did. But first she must stop by the house, and she asked the angel to wait just a moment by the old plum tree. She opened the door to the kitchen, hung up her apron, swept the floor and put away the broom, watered the geraniums and put down a saucer of milk for the cat. Then she closed the door behind her.

Her house was in order, her work was done. She called to the angel. "I'm ready, let's go!"

And off they went to an eternity of being with God without interruption.

Paul Miki
and Charles Lwanga

February 5 and June 3

nce upon a time there were two young men who had no more in common than bananas and baseballs. One, Paul Miki, lived 400 years ago in Japan and the other, Charles Lwanga, lived 300 years later in the African country of Uganda. Everything about them was different—the color of their skin, their language, their food—even the way they combed their hair. For fun, Paul flew a kite and played a bamboo flute; Charles speared fish and beat the drums.

Their lives were separated by oceans and mountains and centuries. Yet I would not doubt that right this moment they are the best of friends in heaven, for they have one strong bond: They belong to a special group of saints we call the martyrs.

Now what is so special about being a martyr? Weren't all the saints martyrs in some fashion or another? Didn't they all give up their comforts and their lives to follow Christ? And didn't they all get to heaven sooner or later?

Yes, but the martyrs got there quicker. The dictionary says that a martyr is one who suffers *keenly* for his or her faith, even choosing to die rather than lose it.

Dying is something we'd just as soon not think about. We know we have to do it *sometime*, like cleaning under our bed or getting a booster shot, and we know that death is our bridge from this life to heaven. But we love this life so much, we hope that bridge stays out of sight. It's like being on a journey and enjoying the journey so much we've forgotten where we're going.

The martyrs knew where they were going. They knew their lives could end quickly and cruelly, usually without warning, simply because they were Christians. They could expect to be torn apart by the lions, thrown into fires, hung from crosses, beheaded, stoned, or thrown off cliffs. It wasn't something you would want to wake up to in the morning. Some of their stories are so gruesome they make us shudder. We'd much rather enjoy the saints who told riddles or moved mountains or made chicken soup and died peacefully in bed at the age of 96.

But the martyrs had absolutely perfect faith that God would get them through the bad moments and would be waiting for them with open arms as they rushed pell-mell across the bridge. How else could they look into the jaws of a ravenous lion with such joy?

These instant saints filled a very special need. Their one blazing moment of courage lit the way for brand-new Christians and for those who may not have heard of Christ at all. The martyrs were seed-saints, Holy Johnny Appleseeds, who shed their blood on soil which needed that nourishment *right then*.

Paul Miki and Charles Lwanga were such seed-saints. Paul was a Japanese Jesuit brother who chose to follow in the footsteps of Francis Xavier, spreading Christ's message in his land. He knew that the missionaries who came across the oceans found his people to be a strange and sometimes confusing race.

The Japanese were most often gentle and courteous. Good manners, they said, is the art of offending no one. Like Bridgid of Ireland, they would give a visitor everything in their desire to please. They had a great love for simplicity and order (Japanese children never had messy bedrooms or left dirty dishes on the table) and nature. A poet could spend years writing about a rose heavy with the morning dew or a chickadee in the lilac bush.

But sometimes they could also kill a servant or enemy or wife just before lunch and sit down to eat without being upset about it.

Japan was a land of hard, unforgiving traditions. Like every land, it needed Christ's love to warm its people's hearts so they might see the cruelty of their ways.

When Francis came to Japan in 1549, the rulers welcomed him and the missionaries who were to follow. But 40 years later the Christians led an uncertain life. Their growing power had frightened the rulers, who decided to do away with them. The Christians at once went into hiding, but it was too late for Paul Miki and 25 other Christians who were his friends. They were captured and condemned to die because they refused to deny that they were Christians.

Paul and his companions were quite a mixed bag of would-be saints. It was as if God had handpicked a bouquet of flowers from different fields. There were Jesuit and Franciscan brothers, young altar boys and old men, a doctor, a servant, an artist and a carpenter—each serving God in a different way and all to die for him the same way.

They were taken to Nagasaki to a spot called the Hill of Wheat, where 26 crosses awaited them. A light covering of snow fell softly, a small comfort of beauty which the Japanese would appreciate. Some of their fellow Christians came out of hiding to offer them gifts of food and wine. Even though eating was not on their minds at that moment, the Christians took bits of fish and sips of wine so they would not offend their friends.

As the soldiers fastened them to the crosses, the Christians started to sing. The three altar boys, in their high-pitched voices, burst forth with these words: "Praise the Lord, all ye children!"

And Paul, in what voice he had left, began to preach to his people. He reminded them he was a true Japanese and that he was being killed simply because he was following Christ. "I thank God it is the reason for which I die," he smiled. "I want to say to you again, ask Christ to help you become as happy as I am. . . . I do not hate my persecutors. I forgive them, as he did. I pray God have pity on them and that my blood fall on this Japan and my brothers as a fruitful rain. . . ."

So also did Charles Lwanga, a young black Christian of Uganda, offer his life as a fruitful rain for the faith in his country. He was a member of the Kabaka's royal household and first learned about Christ from another member, Joseph Mukaso, who was in charge of the royal pages.

When Mwanga, who hated all Christians, became the new Kabaka, he was determined that none of his people would ever become one. When Joseph scolded him for murdering a Protestant missionary, Mwanga accused him of being a Christian spy. When Joseph told him he was not a spy but he was indeed a Christian, the enraged ruler put an end to him by removing his head. That very night Charles was baptized.

Charles quickly took over the care of the 21 young pages. He gathered them together and baptized them, for he had a feeling they were not long for this world. "We shall all go to heaven together," he promised them, "so let us think about how wonderful it will be."

The very next morning, Mwanga ordered Charles and the pages to come before him. "Declare, if you dare, that you are Christians!" he roared.

They stood up and quietly and firmly answered, "Yes, we follow Christ the Lord!"

Mwanga sneered and laughed coarsely. "And how long do you remain Christians, now that I know about you?"

"Forever!" they called out together.

"Till death!" added Kizita, who was 13 and the youngest.

"Very well then, go to your God in that place you call heaven, and good riddance to the lot of you! Put them to the fire," he ordered the executioner.

So they went on their way, a chattering, excited band who seemed more to be going to a wedding feast than their own funeral. A missionary priest from France watched as they passed by and later wrote: "I was not allowed to say a word to them and had to content myself with seeing on their faces. . .the happiness and courage of their hearts."

They were bound and thrown into prison, and for seven days they listened to the sounds of carpenters sawing and hammering and whistling. They knew a large wooden platform was being built on which the Christians were to be burned. Finally they were brought out and each one bound in a mat of woven reeds.

"We shall see whether the God you trust will deliver you from the fire!" laughed Mwanga as he held a flame to the dried reeds. The flame took hold and above the war chants of the soldiers and the and the crackling of the huge fire, the sweet voices of the young martyrs could be heard: "You may burn our bodies but you cannot harm our souls! Jesus is Lord!"

May the voices of Paul and Charles and *all* the martyrs rush like a joyous wind at our back, rolling, pushing, wishing us *Godspeed!* as we totter off to meet the lions—or whatever else may lie in wait around the corner.

Patrick

March 17

here was once a bishop born of a Roman father and a French mother who became the patron saint of Ireland. The Irish, a people of ready wit, say God must be Irish to play such a joke! Well, that we can't prove. What we do know is that the bishop was God's own gift to Ireland and to all of us.

His name was Patricius, son of Calpornius (the way the Irish form a name, that would make him Patrick McAlpern). We know him best as good St. Patrick, the missionary saint who turned the hearts of the pagan Irish to God. He did it so well that now, 15 centuries later, we find it hard to imagine Ireland as a country where people worshiped tree spirits and the gods of sun and moon and thunder. Today Ireland is known as a country of scholars and saints and people who love words almost as well the Word. And you might say it all happened because Patrick was a lazy boy who couldn't abide school.

We're not sure where Patrick was born. It might have been in Scotland or England, or in a coastal town of Wales. Wherever he lived, it was in much comfort and style. His father was a Roman soldier stationed in England, and the family was quite happy in their life in this new land. Their home was like a Roman villa, with tiled floors and baths and gardens and wall hangings. Patrick enjoyed waking in the morning to the sound of waves hitting the shore and the call of sea gulls to get up, get ready, get to school.

89

School was the worm in Patrick's apple. He hated to study. When his mother called up at night and asked if he was doing his homework, he would lie and call back, "Yes, mother, I'm almost finished." And then he would continue whittling his slingshot.

One day when the sun was lovely and warm and shone on the water like a handful of scattered diamonds, Patrick decided he couldn't *bear* to sit in a stuffy classroom and learn about the stars or Latin or God. So instead of taking the road to school, he followed the path that led to the shore. He leaped over tree roots and swung from limbs and pretended he was hiding from the fierce Scots or Picts. They would never catch him! Then he ran along the shore, stopping to pick up small white stones for his slingshot.

Then he froze on the spot. A black pirate ship, captained by Niall of the Nine Hostages, swooped into the cove and made a raid on the village. They grabbed every young man and girl they could find —including Patrick—and carried them screaming on board the creaking ship. Then they set sail for Ireland, a land Patrick knew to be filled with wild men and beasts.

When they reached Ireland the captives were sold in the marketplace. The air was filled with the gentle jabbering of an unknown tongue, Gaelic. Patrick, for the first time in his life, was frightened. Oh, how he wished he were back in his classroom! But God had another school in mind for him. He was sold to Milchu, a chieftain who needed a shepherd for his herd of sheep and swine.

For the next six years, Patrick was that shepherd, tending the animals on the slope of a mountain called Slemish. It was a way of life about which he knew nothing, but he got his wits about him and learned quickly. He built himself a hut and kept a fire going day and night to keep the wolves away. He learned the language and made friends with the people, especially the children of Milchu. In the winter he lived in the kitchen and helped make cheese and butter.

Soon he began to love his life and his solitude. Never before had he thought about God as he did now. Like the Old Testament shepherd, David, he let the Lord become his refuge and his joy. "Constantly,

I used to pray in the daytime," he wrote. "Love of God increased more and more and my faith grew and my spirit was stirred up. . . . Before the day, I was aroused to prayer, in snow and frost and rain, because the spirit was fervent within."

He thought about his old life very seldom now. Then one night in a dream, he heard a voice telling him to fast and pray, for soon he would be going home. Patrick woke and his heart pounded with excitement. It had been so real! So he did fast and pray, and in a few nights he had another dream. The same voice said, "Go now, Patrick, your ship is ready, *go!*"

So Patrick got up and left in the night, taking nothing with him. He walked along the coast, asking kind villagers for food and a bed for the night. He had traveled almost 200 miles and was nearly exhausted when he saw a ship just about ready to leave, and the voice within said, "Here's your ship, Patrick, run!" And he caught it with the help of a crewman who threw him a rope.

Patrick thought his troubles were over. He was on a ship sailing out of Ireland, away from captivity. He was a free man. He was also a strong, healthy young man of 22 and the crew was glad to have him aboard to help. They put up with his talk of God but didn't really listen to him. That was none of their affair.

Three days out to sea, there was a storm of great violence which tossed them about. Finally the boat ran aground on the shores of France. The crew searched for food and water in vain. The sun beat down upon them and many fainted and fell in little heaps in the sand. The captain, who was still standing, laughed weakly and said to Patrick, "Well, Christian, where is your God now? If he is so high and mighty, why doesn't he take care of us? Doesn't he know we are starving?"

Patrick knelt down and prayed with all his heart, "Please, Lord, send some food. And please don't take too long if you want them to believe."

And, wouldn't you know, at that moment a herd of wild pigs came out of the woods. The sailors were overjoyed. They would not die now, they had food. Patrick went into the woods and found a hollow log stuffed with honey and a small tree covered with little red apples. That night by the light of a fire they had pork chops and applesauce.

Patrick said good-bye to the sailors and went his own way. Again, we are not sure, but we think he went to visit his mother's brother, St. Martin of Tours, and then to an island off southern France where he lived in a monastery and studied to be a priest. One night after he was ordained, he again heard a voice in his dream—the same voice he had heard many years ago in Ireland.

It was his guardian angel speaking, showing him an armful of letters. On the top one were the words, *The voice of the Irish*. As Patrick began to read, he heard the sweet, plaintive lilt of Gaelic spoken by the people he knew, calling to him. "We beg you, holy boy, to come and walk once more among us."

Patrick awoke and knew without a doubt that his life now had a definite mission. He was to return to the land where he was once held captive and bring the Irish to the true faith.

When he was in his 40's and a bishop, Patrick finally set sail for Ireland with a band of young and zealous missionaries. As soon as he set foot on shore he began to preach. The pagans, at first afraid, caught the saint's fervor and were converted. Never were people so ready to hear what Christ had to say!

They told Patrick that there would be a gathering of the chieftains and Druid priests at Tara, the castle of the High King Laoghire, to celebrate the birthday of the new year. Here the fire for the new year would be lighted by the Druid priests. On the day before, all the old fires were to be put out and none relighted until the flames from the new one could be seen from Tara.

Now the evening of their festival was also the eve of Easter. Patrick knew that one thing the chieftains respected was a show of courage, and he was not one to be timid. He had been through enough adventures and hardships to make him tough and clever. He was also bold, stubborn and hot-tempered, so if anyone said to him, "You can't build a fire tonight," you can imagine what his answer would be.

So Patrick and his band went up to the top of the Hill of Slade, directly across from Tara, and there "kindled a fire in the nostrils of King Laoghire." The Druids were aghast when they saw the flames of the Christians' Easter fire licking the sky. They hurried to the king and told him he must kill the fire *and* Patrick immediately, "for this fire will blaze forever in our land if it is not put out at once."

The king gave orders to the warriors and priests to storm the Hill of Slade. Up they climbed, wheezing and grunting under the burden of buckets of water, to put out the worrisome fire. But try as they might, even stamping on it and dousing it with earth and sand, the fire would not go out. Patrick and his men knelt down and sang, "Let God arise and let his enemies be scattered!"

The king, who was a very smart man, wondered to himself what manner of man this Patrick was, who would kneel down and sing while his enemies circled about him. And what kind of fire would not go out? He admired Patrick's bravery and ordered him to come to his court the next morning and tell him about this new faith.

The Druid priests were upset and angry. They were quite satisfied with the tree gods and wood nymphs and feared they would be destroyed by Patrick's God. They decided to kill Patrick themselves. The next morning as Patrick and his men made their way to Tara, the Druids hid in ambush along the road. As the singing of the men grew closer, they made ready their spears and clubs. Then they sprang from the bushes—and what did they see?

A doe leading 20 fawns! The Druids fled, fearing a magic spell would be cast upon them if they touched the animals. The song which the deer sang (they were, of course, Patrick and his band) has come down to us as "St. Patrick's Breastplate," a song filled with the saint's trust that if he cast his cares upon the Lord, the Lord would sustain him:

> *I arise today,*
> *God's strength guiding me,*
> *God's might sustaining me,*

God's wisdom directing me,
God's eye looking before me,
God's ear listening to me,
God's word speaking for me,
God's hand protecting me,
The way of God stretching out before me,
The shield of God as my shelter. . . .

King Laoghire never became a Christian, but his queen and the two princesses wanted to become Christians. They could understand everything, they said, except the Blessed Trinity. How could there be three people in one, they asked Patrick?

He reached down and, from the abundance of shamrocks growing underfoot, picked one. "Do you see this little plant?" he asked them. "It is one plant, one stem, but it has three leaves. Three leaves on one stem. And that is the way with the Trinity. God is the stem, the three leaves are the Father, the Son and the Holy Spirit. Now do you understand?" They did, and became Christians on the spot.

From that day on, Patrick never sat still a moment. He traveled the green meadows and hills of Ireland tirelessly for 30 years. He was never deterred by cold or hunger or thirst. He sometimes slept on bare stone with a wet cloak about him, a rock for his pillow. It seemed as if God's light did surround and protect him, for he almost single-handedly changed the hearts of the Irish with Christ's truth. And it was done without bloodshed.

There was just one instance of injury, an accident for which Patrick was very sorry. When he was baptizing King Angus of Cashel, he brought the spike of his bishop's staff down sharply, like an exclamation point, to emphasize a point in his sermon. The staff went right through the king's big toe.

The king said nothing although his eyebrows shot up quickly and his face turned a shade pale. When Patrick found out what he had done, he was all sympathy and bound up the bloody toe himself.

"Why didn't you tell me?" he asked the king.

"I thought it was part of the ceremony," the king answered bravely.

Patrick laughed, "You may have to give up some things to be a Christian, but not your *toe!*"

Patrick baptized 120,000 souls by his own hand, founded 700 churches, ordained 5,000 priests and 370 bishops. Some say he was able to accomplish so much because he was such a practical saint and traveled equipped for everything. The Boy Scouts should have him as their special saint, they add, because he certainly knew how to *be prepared.* He would come with a household of 12 clerics (native Irish boys who were going to become priests), an assistant bishop, a chaplain, a judge for legal matters, a strong man, bell-ringers, blacksmiths, cooks, brewers, gardeners, bricklayers, cowherds, carpenters, masons, artists, seamstresses and, of course, a poet and a musician.

After he had baptized the people of a village, Patrick would look for a spot he felt was right for their church. His household would come to a halt and in a clatter of pots and hammers and bells and harps set to work digging the foundation. Blacksmiths forged nails and door-hinges. Artists and coppersmiths gave beauty to the altar and vessels while seamstresses embroidered the linens. When the church was ready for its first celebration of Mass, Patrick would give it a name and leave the new parish in the hands of a young priest. Then the household would travel on and do the same thing in another spot the next day.

This is how Patrick spent his life. In 30 years, all of Ireland became Christian—which amazed even Patrick. He was humble enough to know that only God, working through him, could do this. He wished—oh, how he wished!—that he had not been such a lazy student. If he were a scholar, he thought, he could have done even greater things.

Nonetheless, God used him for extraordinary work. It could be that God knew he could depend upon Patrick, through thick and thin, hill and bog. Patrick was reliable, he was steadfast.

If you have ever read Hans Christian Andersen's story, *The Steadfast Tin Soldier,* you may recognize some of his qualities in Patrick. He too was brave, single-minded and absolutely certain that one day he would be united with his one true Love. Every morning he prayed that God would keep him steadfast:

May the strength of God guide me this day,
and may his power preserve me.
May the wisdom of God instruct me,
the ear of God hear me,
the Word of God give sweetness to my speech,
the hand of God defend me.
And may I follow the way of God!

Patrick is the saint for all who would stand fast and hold tight to God's Word, no matter what. Patrick will help us to overcome the pirates and Druids and shipwrecks of our own lives with no trouble at all.

And if your name happens to be Patrick McAlpern, just think what he will do for *you!*

Joseph

March 19

oseph, they say,
Was quiet and good,
He prayed all the while
He whittled his wood.

He was gentle and just
And quite ordinary,
This carpenter who married
The young virgin Mary.

'Twould be simple, he thought,
Their way of life,
In Bethlehem's nest
As husband and wife.

This was all he asked,
All he'd expect,
But God had plans for Joseph
He didn't suspect.

He whispered them to Gabriel,
Who mentioned them to Mary,
Who carried the secret
Like a pit in a cherry.

But no one told Joseph,
Who was left in the dark,
Fumbling for the answer
To a stubborn question mark.

Then in a dream an angel
Said nothing was amiss—
The Son that Mary carried
Was simply God's, not his.

"How can this be?"
He puzzledly exclaimed,
The angel only shrugged,
"Because God so proclaimed!"

Surely, there were others
Of the House of David's tree,
Who could serve a royal child
More appropriately!

The angel reassured him
In no uncertain voice:
"Joseph, you are handpicked,
You're the Father's choice!"

So he went about his work,
This ordinary man,
Hammering his life
Into the Master's plan.

And Mary and Jesus
And himself, all three,
Were a family as special
As the Blessed Trinity.

He went to the fields
To show Jesus how
To cast the seeds
And work the plow

And prune the vines
And budge the boulder
And find the sheep
Lost in the alder

And swing the axe
With one good stroke
To fell the cedar,
Pine and oak.

He showed his Son
That a house must be built
On solid rock
And not on silt.

They worked in the shop
And planed the beams
And made a wagon
And joined the seams

And fashioned wheels
And baskets and benches,
All with a saw
And nails and wrenches.

They hummed and prayed
And measured and whistled,
While wood chips curled
Under their chisels,

Then went home weary
When work was done
To Mary and chowder
And cinnamon buns.

The years flew by
As he stood in the wings,
Coaching his Son
For greater things.

Of where he died,
We have no notion,
Or whether he lies
In hillock or ocean,

But they say on Good Friday
When Jesus died,
Joseph ascended
To the Other Side.

God hugged him tight
As a long-lost brother,
Rather it was more
One Father to another.

Despite all this, he
Would ever find it odd
That a man with shavings in his beard
Should raise the Son of God.

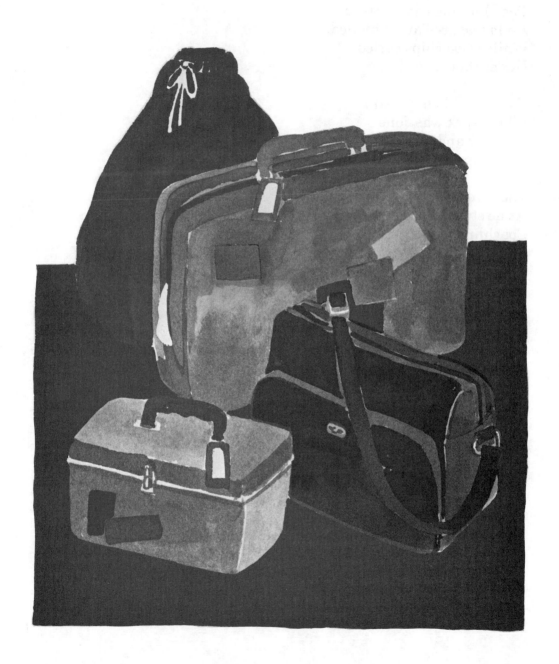

Saints for the Journey

Lent/Easter

The people you will meet in this section have gathered for a journey. Their stories—and ours—are part of the long journey the human race has been struggling for centuries to complete. It began with God, though it quickly twisted and turned far away from him. He waits at its end, eager to say, "The road ends here," and to hold out his hand to grasp his children's. Only then will all of us drop our tattered luggage of aches and pains and blistered hearts.

Just once there was a man who came from God and made the journey home to him without ever tripping over the potholes or getting caught in brambles. His name, of course, is Jesus; his journey provides the roadmap for all the weary travelers. With the rest we follow him through the seasons of Lent and Easter, turning back to glimpse the people from whom he came, trudging up the steep sides of Calvary behind him, hurrying ahead to spy the bright light of Easter morn and running to carry the Good News about the journey's end to the rest of the world.

In this section are some of the people who travel with us. They trod the same road even though they came from different lands at different times and had little in common except that they met the Lord along the way and when he said, "Come, follow me," they did.

We too are on a journey. We carry our own bags of weaknesses: weak hearts or ankles or brains, sharp tongues that cut as deep as razor blades. We may stumble and trip over our untied shoelaces or get dizzy and see stars.

But we mustn't be discouraged! God has given us his Son who will stay with us uphill and down, and his saints who will guide us as surely as signposts. They will provide the flashlights and slickers and Band-Aids, and they will point us in the direction of the rainbow.

Adam and Eve

nce upon a time, there was nothing. And no one. There were no mothers or fathers. There was no you sitting in a chair reading this book. There was no can of tuna fish or jar of peanut butter on the shelf because there were no tuna fish or peanuts.

There was only God and darkness. He was wrapped in it; he looked up at it and down at it. After this had been going on for billions of years, God decided it was time for a change. Perhaps he had too much love to hold inside him.

You know that when you love, you can't keep it to yourself. You want to share your joy with the whole world. God too found it hard to keep happiness to himself, so he thought he would create a family of children in his own image to share in all the good things he had in mind for them.

But before there could be a family, there had to be a world. One morning God told himself, "Today's the day! First, I will let there be light." and he divided the time into light and darkness and called the light *day* and the darkness *night*. Then he created air, space, the heavens, and the stars and sun and moon and planets. How he must have enjoyed watching the stars twinkle that first night and the dawn streaked red with the first sunrise the next morning!

(We don't know exactly how God created the world.

Whether he snapped his fingers and there was a whale or mushroom or Adam, or whether it took thousands of years from the explosion of that first spark into the darkness, we can only imagine. However he did it, we know that spark came from God's love.)

Then he made the seas and oceans and the earth which is our home now. And then, because the ground needed something pretty and green to cover it, he made the grasses and shrubs and herbs and trees. Now the earth was restful and lovely, but too quiet. So he brought forth all kinds of birds and fishes and everything that crept and crawled. Then he added all the animals who would live on the earth—monkeys and horses and dinosaurs and gazelles and foxes—oh, what a bustling place the earth was!

Still, it wasn't complete. God chose the most beautiful spot in this brand new world and made it into a garden. He called it Eden, which means *delight,* and it was a true garden of delights. He filled it with every fruit, flower and vegetable you can imagine and some you can't, and he put a river of the purest crystal clear water running right down the middle of the garden. He checked the temperature and made it just right so nothing would ever burn or freeze or sweat.

It was time to make his family. God took a handful of dust and from it he formed the first man and breathed the breath of life into him. God called him Adam. Then God thought that it wasn't good for Adam to be alone, so he made him a companion he could love as God loved him.

He put Adam into a very deep sleep and then took a rib from his side. He worked dust around it until he had made another creature in his likeness. He called her a woman and named her Eve. He brought her to Adam and told them to "increase and multiply and fill the earth and rule over the fishes and birds and all living things that move upon the earth. I have given you every herb and tree and plant. I have given you the whole world!"

Adam and Eve lived in a happy innocence in the Garden of Eden. Everything was perfect. They were never sick or tired or hungry. They didn't know what it meant to fear or hate or lie or be greedy. Nor did the animals disagree or hurt one another. The fawn huddled up to the tiger when her mother was busy, while the white rabbit played leapfrog with the red fox. And the black cat never forgot a piece of cheese for the mouse's supper.

Adam and Eve talked with the animals and treated them as friends. They trimmed the lawn and pruned the plum trees and made rock gardens. They picked lemon grass and chamomile flowers for tea and invited God to dinner, after which they would stroll in the garden in the cool of the evening and talk about the day.

God gave them the job of naming everything. This took many days and months (they even had to name the days and months) because nothing on earth had been named except Adam and Eve. So each day they went off onto different paths and came back for dinner with long lists in their hands.

"Mine first, Adam, listen to what I found." And Eve would chant excitedly, "Poppy, hyacinth, chokecherries, eggplant, mustard—"

And Adam would interrupt, "Castor oil, jelly beans, alarm clock, worms, brussels sprouts, and a blue heron."

"Hippopotamus!" said Eve.

"Rhinoceros!" said Adam.

One day Adam named the stars and planets and bugs, and Eve named the colors and flowers and birds. The Lord was pleased with his children and how they were taking care of the garden on their own. He had given them no rules except for one. He told them they must never eat from a certain tree which grew in the middle of Eden.

"You may eat anything from any of the other plants or trees here, but not of the Tree of Good and Evil. For the day that you do, you will die."

Adam and Eve did not understand what it meant to die. They had no way of knowing, being the first people on earth. But they knew that they loved God and so they obeyed him. They left the tree alone.

One afternoon as Eve rested under an apricot tree after naming numbers up to 100, a sleepy-eyed serpent slithered up the tree, coiled himself around a low branch, and hung down over her. He stuck out his tongue and called her name slyly.

Eve looked up. "Hello, serpent, what's on your mind today?"

"Oh, I was just thinking," he hissed, "isn't it time for you to rest and have a bite to eat after all your hard work?"

"I think I will. Thanks, serpent, for reminding me." And she reached up and picked a plump apricot. She was very pleased for having named the fruit *apricot* because it tasted as sweet and velvety golden as it sounded.

"Oh, don't bother with that plain old apricot! Why don't you try those special apples on that tree over there?" And the serpent pointed to the Tree of Good and Evil which had been forbidden to them by God.

"I couldn't do that. You *know* we may eat anything in Eden but that. God said not to eat it or even touch it, or we will die—whatever that means. I don't like the sound of it."

"Nonsense," said the serpent, "you mustn't believe such things. Do you know why God doesn't want you to eat those apples? Because then you'll be as smart as he is and know everything there is to know."

"Look at me," he boasted, "I ate from that tree just this morning and I'm not dead, am I? I'm fit as a fiddle and raring to go. There's no one in this garden as smart as I am. But if you eat from it, too, then we'll both be the smartest creatures in the world. And then we can tell *God* what to do!"

Eve said nothing but, "Well ..." She wished Adam were here. Those apples looked so good. She wondered if Adam had named them yet.

"McIntosh," said the serpent in her ear.

"Well," thought Eve, "he must be smart if he can read my mind."

"Ask me anything, anything," he stuck out his tongue again, "and I'll tell you the answer. All because I eat an apple a day from that tree. Come on, try one, just one little bite. God won't see you."

Eve really wanted that apple now. Just one little bite. She ran over and carefully plucked the deep purple-red apple. She took a bite so deep it crackled with juicy crispness. It was *so* good.

She called Adam and said, "Adam, you must taste this apple. You've never had any so good." So Adam did, and ate up everything but the stem.

When she told him from which tree she had picked it, Adam felt something he hadn't known before—fear. And then they looked at each other and for the first time saw that they were not wearing clothes. And the second thing he felt, and Eve too, was shame. She quickly gathered up some fig leaves, sewed them together, and made the first underwear.

They heard the voice of the Lord calling to them, and they hid behind the trees, hoping he would not see them.

God called to Adam, "Adam? Where are you?"

Adam come out from the trees, hanging his head. "I hid myself, Lord, because I knew I was naked."

"Who told you that you were naked?" asked God. "How did you know unless you had eaten from the tree that was forbidden to you?"

"It wasn't my fault, Lord," said Adam quickly. "Eve, whom you gave to me as my friend, gave me the fruit and told me to eat it."

"And you ate it?"

"Well, she said it was all right, just one little bite."

Then God said to Eve, who was still behind the tree, "What is this you have done, Eve?"

"It wasn't my fault, Lord. The serpent tempted me to take just one apple and said that I would be as smart as you if I ate it. But I took just one little bite so I'd be just a *little* smarter, not a whole lot..."

God heard the serpent snickering up in the tree. He sighed. How quickly Paradise had been lost! For a moment of disobedience his two creations, whom he wanted to enjoy and love, had thrown away eternity as God's children.

He told the snake, "You have won this time, but oh, what you have lost! Because you have tempted my son and daughter, you shall crawl on your belly and eat dust all the days of your life. I shall make the woman and her children enemies of you through the years, and they shall bruise your head."

To Adam he said, "Because you listened to Eve and ate the apple, the ground shall be cursed for you. It will bring forth thorns and thistles. By the sweat of your brow you will earn your bread and raise your children—until you die and your bodies return to dust."

He was still their friend. He clothed them in skins of animals to cover their nakedness, but he could not let them stay in the Garden. Now they would have to go out into the world beyond, to work and feel pain and weariness. God would not be close by, as when they used to talk with him and watch a hummingbird drink in the fragrance of the honeysuckle bush.

As they left, an angel with a flaming sword stood guard by the Tree of Life, and then the gate closed and heavy thick vines of bittersweet and wild grape immediately grew and wove themselves into a curtain that could never be parted. Paradise was gone from sight forever.

They looked back at their home with sadness, and then began the first steps of their journey, and ours as well. Now, so many years later, we are still a-journeying, but unlike Adam and Eve, we are not alone. God sent us his Son Jesus as our guide and comforter.

And because he came and died for us, a new Paradise is waiting!

In the meantime, be very careful of serpents who offer you apples.

Noah

nce upon a time there lived a man named Noah who built a boat in his backyard. It wasn't a sailboat he could use on the lake, or a rowboat to fish from on the river, or a canoe to paddle in up the stream. It was a boat so big it looked like a three-story apartment house. It was the biggest boat ever seen in the world at that time. And it took 100 years to build.

Noah was 600 years old when he began to build the boat, which was a very ordinary age for people to be at that time. (He had a relative named Methuselah who lived for 969 years.) Although the world was still very young, the children and the great-great-great-grandchildren of Adam and Eve had filled it with many people.

Sad to say, the human race must not have learned anything from their first parents' punishment, because they all turned out to be a mean and wicked lot. They were selfish and cruel and stole and lied and paid no attention to God. Even their animals hated and killed each other.

God looked at the mess the world was in and grieved that he had ever made it. He was even sorrier he had made people. Out of all these descendants of Adam he could find only one good, just man, and his name was Noah. This man tried time and time again to talk to his neighbors, to coax them to be sorry for their meanness. He told them it was never too late to start over, living to serve God. But they laughed

and hooted and snickered over that crazy Noah and kept on hitting each other over the head with clubs.

Finally God decided that the only thing to do was to start over again himself. He would wash the earth clean of these wicked men and women. "I will bring a flood of waters upon the earth to destroy all flesh under heaven that has the breath of life. And everything on the earth shall die," he said.

Everything and everyone but Noah. One day, when Noah was busy putting new hinges on the barn door, God called to him, "Noah, you have long walked with me. Now listen to me. The time has come when all the men and women on earth are to be destroyed because they have been so wicked. But you and your family shall be saved, because you alone are trying to do right."

He told Noah exactly what he must do. Noah was to build a boat, or ark, which would be 500 feet long and 80 feet wide and 50 feet high. It would be three stories high, with rooms and stairways and windows in the top floor and one door in the side. It would have a flat bottom. Noah was to start building it now of cypress wood, which was light, and it was to be covered with pitch inside and out so there would be no little cracks.

"You shall come into the ark with your wife and sons and their wives," said God, "and out of every living thing, you shall bring two of each sort, male and female, birds and creeping things as well. And take up some of every kind of food you eat, so you shall have nourishment to keep you a long time."

Noah sat quietly, very puzzled. God had chosen him alone to be saved from a flood. This flood would wipe out the earth, and Noah and his family would be the only ones left to start a new world. How, he wondered, should he tell his family, and would they believe him?

He needn't have worried for as soon as he told them of God's command and promise, his sons and their wives jumped up and said, "Let's get to work!" Noah's wife was a little harder to convince. She could imagine all the work she would have to do, preparing food for such a journey, not only for the family but also for all those animals!

And suppose Noah had just imagined all this. The neighbors would really have a good laugh.

The neighbors did laugh once they got wind of what Noah was up to out back. As soon as they heard him and his sons, Shem, Ham and Japheth, hammering and singing and sawing, they came around and gawked. When he told them what he was doing, they burst into rude laughter. That crazy old man, building a monster of a boat with not a lake or river or stream for hundreds of miles around!

Pretty soon it would become so big he couldn't even get it out of the backyard, they said. It became part of their daily fun to run on down to Noah's and see what the old fool was up to. The men would snicker and agree that "Nutty Noah was out to lunch." And the little girls would swing their jump ropes and chant mean things like:

Ring around a rosy robin,
Nutty Noah's off his noggin!

But Noah just kept hammering and sawing and feeling sorry for all of them. While the men were working outside, the women were in the kitchen drying apples and figs and raisins and dates and roasting almonds and pumpkin seeds. Then they mixed them with oats and bran and wheat germ and made 365 packages of granola.

They poured wheat and rye kernels for sprouting into stone jars and water into goat skins. They packed salt and sauerkraut and honey into covered crocks. Noah's wife baked many loaves of good hard pumpernickel bread for her husband and set aside one dozen jars of wild raspberry jam for their Sunday breakfasts.

She was getting tired. It was work all day, and then she never got to see her husband because he worked late by moonlight. It had been years since Noah chopped the first tree for wood for the ark. She nagged him to get done so they could have a decent night's sleep.

"I swear, Noah," she would sigh. "Why do you take so long? You should have had this ark done years ago. You're as slow as molasses running uphill!"

To which Noah would reply, patiently, "I must do it perfectly. This is no ordinary boat, you know. It was designed by God.

When the time comes, you'll be glad I wasn't sloppy."

The time came just as he finished putting the trim on the third-floor windows. God told Noah to gather the animals and birds and crawling things. That wasn't as difficult as it might seem, because the animals had a sense of the coming storm and wanted to be where they would be safe. So Noah called and they came and filed into the ark happily, two by two, he and she, ant-eaters and zebras, elephants and peacocks, racoons and giraffes.

Just as Noah latched and bolted the door in the side of the ark and nailed it shut, a little drizzle of rain began to fall. The sky grew very black and God called out from heaven, "Be of good cheer, Noah. No matter what happens, you will be safe in my care."

It rained harder and everyone in the ark could hear it pelting against the sides of the ark. It rained all day and all night and the next day and the next. It rained for 40 days and 40 nights, and the ark began to move. The wind and water lifted it up and it sailed over the meadow, over the homes of Noah's neighbors who had laughed at him, and over the hills and mountains. The waters covered everything. There was nothing left alive on earth except Noah and his family and the animals in the ark.

The animals had their own beds and plenty of hay and grain and water. The birds nested in the rafters. And the creeping things went where they wanted. Sometimes, when the boat would pitch and toss during the storm, the smaller animals would be jolted across the room to land in the lap of an elephant. But for the most part, they all put up with each other beautifully.

The rats and skunks and porcupines promised to behave themselves and not offend any of the others. Since they were all in this together to be saved, they would not chew the beams or steal food or do anything to make the trip unpleasant. They ate all the garbage, which made everyone happy.

For five months it rained and the ark tossed in and out of the angry waves. Noah went down to visit the animals every day to keep them calm and in good spirits. He certainly didn't want the elephant to get restless. One morning Noah woke up and heard a strange sound: no rain. Then he felt the boat shudder and heard a scraping sound. He opened the window and saw that they were sitting on top of a mountain—and there they sat for four months.

Finally Noah decided the time had come to explore the situation. He called the dove and she flew up and out the open window. Noah hoped she would bring back some sign to show that land was nearby. But she was back by evening with nothing to show, for there was no dry spot on earth for her to roost.

Noah waited a week, and then opened the window and let her go off to find land again. And this time she did. She returned before evening with a sprig of an olive branch in her beak. Noah caressed the dove and kissed her. He was so happy. Not only had the rain stopped but the water had gone down enough so the tips of trees could be seen.

Once more, a week later, he sent the dove out. This time she did not come back, so Noah knew she had found seeds for food and a tree for rest.

It had taken many months for the water to drain away into the gound, even with the rain stopped; but finally, a year after they had anxiously hurried into the boat that rainy day, Noah opened the door of the ark and he and his family and the animals ran joyously out into the sunshine.

The first thing Noah did, after he had stretched his arms and body to soak in the warmth of the sun, was to build an altar and offer a sacrifice to God for bringing them back to dry land safely.

And God, in return, told Noah how pleased he was. He said, "I will never again destroy the earth on account of people, no matter how bad they may be. From this moment on, no flood shall ever again cover the earth, but the seasons of spring, summer, fall and winter shall remain without change. I give you the earth! You shall be the rulers of the ground and of every living thing upon it."

Just then, a beautiful rainbow hung in the sky, and the red and blue and green and yellow rays shone onto the raindrops caught in a just-spun spiderweb. They sparkled like tiny colored jewels. God told Noah that whenever he and his family should see the rainbow, they would remember that God had placed it in the sky over the clouds as a sign of his promise to love and remember the earth and the people on it.

So whenever you see a rainbow, usually after a stormy time, remember God's promise to Noah. Remember it is God's sign, telling you he cares about you and you are not to worry about anything. That is why rainbows bring that sudden rush of surprised joy to our hearts.

We almost can't believe the beauty of those gentle colors arched across the sky as they join earth at one end with heaven at the other. Maybe that's what the pot of gold at the end of the rainbow is — heaven!

Abraham

here was once a very old man named Abraham upon whom God played a joke. It made Abraham laugh so hard he fell off his rocker when he heard it. He rolled around and hooted and cackled and drummed his heels so hard on the floor his very old bones almost snapped. His wife Sarah laughed just as hard, but she was more sensible and stood up as she chuckled into her hankie.

Long before they started laughing, God had picked them out to share in his heavenly sense of humor. This wasn't because of Abraham's great closetful of jokes but because of his great trust in a loving God. Abraham didn't think of God as a far-off, fearful being with long-flowing white hair and a frown. God was his good friend.

Abraham and Sarah lived in Chaldea, a country in the Middle East. He was a kind old man, generous and pleasant to his neighbors. But in his heart he wasn't happy. Because his love for God was so deep, he couldn't live comfortably anyplace where he couldn't show that love. In his country everyone about him worshipped the moon and stars and sun. Although he didn't say anything to them, Abraham knew this was wrong. He knew they sould be praying instead to the God who had *created* all these marvelous natural things.

119

So Abraham talked to God about it. They often talked together and discussed the weather and the crops and the wife, as good friends do. We don't know if Abraham actually heard words coming down from heaven. Most likely he felt them very deeply in his heart. One thing is for sure: Whatever God said to do, Abraham did without a question or doubt.

When he asked God what he should do about living in the midst of moon-worshippers, God said, "Come out of this place, Abraham, and I will take you to another land."

So Abraham and Sarah packed up their sun hats and winter pajamas, his garden tools and her favorite tin for date pudding, and rounded up their sheep and goats. They were on their way to wherever the Lord directed.

For a while they lived as nomads, wanderers, stopping here and there whenever they found water for themselves and the animals. They would pitch their tent, made of curtains woven from goat's hair, and stay until the grass and water had been used up.

Finally they came to a lovely spot in the country called Canaan, which we now know as the Holy Land. The fields were not just one big patch of green, but different shades like a patchwork quilt. And the palm trees hung low with heavy clusters of golden red dates, which filled Sarah's heart with delight.

God said to Abraham, "This is it, Abraham. Marvelous things will happen to you here. You will become a rich and respected chieftain, loved by all. And all because you have loved *me*! I am the Almighty God and you shall walk before me and be perfect. You will be the father of many nations and the ancestor of kings."

Naturally, Abraham was overwhelmed at the thought of such things happening to him. He didn't know how it would happen, but if God said it would, then it would.

It did, and Sarah and Abraham knew they had been given the best possible place for them to live. Every now and then, though, one small question would flit across Abraham's mind. Just how was he to become the father of nations when he didn't have any children? And

120

since he was 100 years old and Sarah was 90, he didn't expect that he would ever become a father. The time for that was long past.

God heard this question, even though Abraham quickly put it out of his mind as soon as he realized he was asking it. So the Lord said to the old man, "Sit down, Abraham, I want to tell you something. I am going to bless you and Sarah. I am going to give you a son. I will bless Sarah and she shall be the mother of nations, and the kings of peoples shall come from her."

And what did Abraham do when he heard this? He fell onto the floor laughing. This was the best joke yet! He thought God was having fun with him, but he didn't mind. God waited for his laughter to die down and repeated:

"Sarah, your wife, will bear a son and you shall call him Isaac." Since *isaac* was the word for laughter, Abraham was *certain* this was a joke.

He went and told Sarah who laughed too, but quietly to herself. The Lord heard her anyway and said to her, "Why are you laughing, Sarah? Is anything too hard for God? Is anything impossible? When the seasons come around, you shall have a son!"

Then Sarah, who didn't want God to think her disrespectful, said, "I didn't laugh, Lord."

"Yes, you did."

"Didn't!"

"Did!"

And Sarah let it go at that because she knew God was right.

When Isaac was born, Sarah laughed again—and out loud this time. "God made me laugh. Now everyone who hears this shall laugh with me, this time with joy!" And so they became a family, this old couple with the new baby, a very special family by the grace of God.

A few years went by happily until one morning when God called to his friend Abraham.

"Here I am, Lord," he answered.

"I want you to take Isaac, whom you love so, and go to the mountain I will show you. There please offer him as sacrifice to me."

121

Abraham turned pale and felt as though the breath had been knocked from him. He suddenly felt 200 years old. His heart ached, his mind was stunned. He looked at his shaking hands. How could he use them to take the life of his son?

Even though it is hard to believe, people in those days did offer animals and human beings as sacrifices to their gods. They built altars of stone and earth, placed their live offerings upon it, killed them and then put fire to the altar to make a "burnt offering." Very often parents gave up their children in this way.

Abraham knew of these sacrifices but he never thought such a cruel thing would be asked of him. The God he knew was one who loved life and did not destroy it. And why, after going to all the trouble of giving him a son in his old age and telling him he would be the father of nations, would God take this promise away?

But Abraham said, as always, "Yes, Lord." He would not disobey God. If God asked for this sacrifice of Abraham's dearest son, then it must be done.

So he packed a donkey with wood for the fire, and with two servants and Isaac walking by his side, he started on his journey to the mountain. For two days they walked and when they reached the foot of the mountain God had shown him, Abraham told the servants to wait while he and Isaac went to the top to worship.

"When we are finished," he said, "we will come back down to you." With all his heart Abraham believed that if God took Isaac from him, then he would somehow bring him back to life.

When they had reached the top and built an altar for the sacrifice, Isaac asked, "Father, we have the wood, but where is the lamb for the offering?"

And Abraham, trying to cover the sadness in his voice, answered, "My son, God will provide a lamb for our burnt offering."

Isaac said nothing, but he must have understood that it was he who would be the lamb. How terrible it must have been for them both—for Abraham to see the life of his son snuffed out by his own hand, and for Isaac to know that he was to be the sacrifice!

Abraham tied Isaac's hands and feet and laid him on the altar they had built. He closed his eyes and raised his hand with the knife to kill his son. Suddenly, he heard a voice call out: "Abraham! Abraham!" And there in the heavens, he saw a towering angel.

Abraham, sobbing, answered, "Here I am, Lord!"

And the angel said, "Do not lay your hand on the boy, and do no harm to him. Now God knows that you love him more than you love your only son, and that you are obedient to God."

You can imagine how happy both father and son were to be able to go down the mountain and back home *alive* to be a family again. Before they left the mountaintop, God told Abraham how pleased he was to see how much Abraham loved him. Because of this, God said, he would bless Abraham.

"I will multiply your children and your children's children as the stars in heaven and the sands on the seashore," he promised.

So Abraham, through Isaac, would be the father of nations after all, and among his descendants would be the Son of a King who would tell the world: "My Father is the God of Abraham and the God of laughter!"

From that time on Abraham and those who came after him never offered a human sacrifice. When God stopped him from killing Isaac, Abraham saw that life does not have to be destroyed to show our love for God.

Now we know that we worship our Lord better when we make "burnt offerings" of ourselves. That doesn't mean we play with matches and burn our fingers. It means we offer up what is dear to us— our time, our tempers, our toothbrush, our having the last word. It means doing nice things for people who aren't particularly nice and being pleasant when we feel ugly.

It means when God calls, we say, "Here I am, Lord!"—and get ready to laugh.

Moses

Once upon a time, there was a prophet named Moses who spent all of his life going on a journey. Since he lived to be 120 years old, it was a very *long* journey. And it was not the kind of trip you make to get to Grandma's for Thanksgiving.

It was a tiring and hot and frightening journey, filled with pain and hunger and thirst and snakes and locusts and boils and thunder and hail and death. And you couldn't count the number of blistered heels. Yet Moses kept on. He knew where he was going and why. He knew God had chosen him to keep his promise to Abraham that his children would one day inherit the Promised Land of Canaan, or Israel.

These children were the Hebrews, or Israelites, who were living as slaves in the land of Egypt. At one time they had been invited to come to Egypt and enjoy the good life there by the Pharaoh, or king, and so they did. But now a new Pharaoh ruled, one who disliked and feared the Hebrews. They had followed God's command to increase and multiply so well, there were now almost more of them than Egyptians, and the Pharaoh was afraid they might take over his country.

So he began to treat them harshly. They became slaves to the Egyptians and they were forced to build cities right from scratch: They had to gather the straw to make the bricks that would make the great buildings that helped make Egypt the center of culture and learning. They had to work from the dark before dawn to the dark after sunset.

The Pharaoh thought if he worked them more than they could bear, they would die. But God was with the Hebrews. He gave them the strength to withstand all kinds of work and weather and to thrive and grow even healthier.

The Pharaoh was really worried. Pretty soon there would be more slaves than masters, and he didn't want to think what might happen then. So he ordered all Hebrew boy-babies to be killed at birth. One mother to whom a son had just been born decided she could not possibly obey such an order, and even though she knew she risked her own life, she hid her beautiful child for three months.

Finally, she knew he was getting too big to keep in dark corners and under the bed. His cooing and gurgling and crying for his dinner were too loud. She could no longer say to neighbors, "Oh, that's just those noisy chickens!" Sadly she decided that she must part with him if he were to have a chance to live.

She wrapped him tightly in a basket she had woven herself and covered him with a blanket made from her shawl. With tears in her eyes, she gave him to his sister Miriam. She told the young girl to take him down to the edge of the Nile River and hide him among the cattails. Here, she hoped, some kind person would find him and take him home. "Goodbye, my little one," she whispered as she kissed him. "You'll never remember me, but know that I love you."

Miriam ran quickly with the basket in her arms and set it carefully in the thickest bunch of cattails near the shore. She hid behind a large bush not too far away to see what would happen. Soon she heard some women laughing and running down to the river, eager for the morning bath. One was the princess, the young daughter of the Pharaoh, who was as kind as her father was cruel.

Just as her toe touched the water, the princess heard a sound in the weeds and she turned her head quickly. One had to be careful when bathing in the river. There were snakes and snapping turtles and alligators who lived there too. She listened without moving and her eyes followed the whimpering sound until she spied the basket. She hurried over to it, for she was a curious young princess. She lifted the shawl and

then smiled with delight. What an incredible sight!

A baby, just beginning to cry and rubbing his fists into his mouth, looked up at her. "This must be a Hebrew baby," she thought. "Some poor mother has put him here, hoping he would find a good home. Well," she said to herself, "he has!"

She knew all about what was happening to the Hebrew babies. She knew how her father felt about the Hebrews but she paid no attention to how he would feel if she brought one home. She was her father's favorite and she could have just about anything she wanted. And she wanted this very special baby she had found.

"Well, little one, I think I'll call you *Moses,* because I drew you out of the water. How would you like to be my own little son and grow up in the palace?"

Miriam was so excited she jumped up out of the bushes and forgot about being afraid. She ran to the princess and asked if she'd like a nurse to help her care for the child.

"Why yes I would, little girl. Do you know of someone?"

Miriam said she knew *just* the right woman, and she ran to get her mother. So the mother who gave her baby away in the morning had him back in the evening, if only for a short time. She took care of Moses until he was old enough to live at the palace. She was satisfied that now he would live and have a fine home.

Moses grew up as an Egyptian prince of the royal house. He learned about astronomy and music and science. He even had his own royal cat, which he enjoyed and cared for but did not worship as the Egyptians did. Moses knew he was a child of Israel and would worship only the one real God.

As he grew older, he found it harder to keep his feelings about the Pharaoh's cruelty to the Hebrews to himself. One day, as he watched a Hebrew slave being beaten by his angry master, he became so angry he killed the Egyptian and buried him in the sand. The word spread and soon the Pharaoh heard the story; and from that moment on, Moses' life was in danger.

He would have to leave the country, leave forever his life of pleasant comforts and enjoyments, leave the two women who had been mothers to him. But, he sighed, what did all those good things matter if he had to turn his back on his people's suffering and pretend he wasn't one of them?

So he fled Egypt in the night and wandered to a wild and desolate land called Midian, where he would be safe. He stopped wearily at a well, thanking God for both his escape and this well that promised cool water, before trying to decide where to go next. While he sat washing his sore feet, seven sisters came up to the well to draw water for their father's sheep. Moses leaped up to help them and did not stop until every animal was content.

The sisters were so grateful they asked him to come home and have supper with them. Their father Jethro, pleased with this young man who had been so polite to his daughters, asked Moses to stay with them, and he did. He became a shepherd like Jethro, and they worked well together and enjoyed each other's company. In time, Moses married one of the seven sisters, Zipporah, and for 40 years they lived a quiet and happy life in Midian.

It was as if his past life in Egypt had never happened. Every now and then he thought of the Hebrews who were still slaves there, but he didn't know what he could do for them. He wondered if God had forgotten about them.

One morning he led his flock up the mountain at Horeb. As he sat down to think and watch the flight of birds and listen to their calls, he saw a small green bush beside him burst into flame. It didn't happen one branch at a time but all at once, in a sudden *poof!* He jumped up to get his goatskin filled with water to put it out. How did it start so suddenly, he wondered. Was the sun so hot and the tree so dry it had to burn?

But it was burning very strangely. The bush did not crackle and shrivel up into a black, brittle skeleton. Every branch and leaf shone through the fire still green and fresh. He went closer. And then a voice came from the bush:

"Moses! Moses!"

And Moses answered, "Here I am, Lord," just as Abraham had done years before.

"Take off your sandals, Moses," said the voice, "for the place where you are standing is holy ground. I am the God of your fathers, the God of Abraham, Isaac and Jacob!"

Moses was frightened and hid his face in his robe.

And then the voice said, "I have seen the affliction of my people who are in Egypt and have heard their cry, for I know their sorrows. I am going to deliver them and bring them into a good land flowing with milk and honey. Come now, and I will send you back to Pharaoh, that you may bring your people out of Egypt!"

Moses couldn't believe his ears. After all this time he had been away from them, God had chosen him to go back to Egypt to set his people free.

But Moses hesitated. He told the Lord he didn't think he could do the job. In the first place, he couldn't talk right. He would get mixed-up and say things backwards or stutter. Sometimes he was so slow in talking people fell asleep between his words.

But God said, "Who has made people dumb or eloquent, seeing or blind? Go, and I will take care of your mouth and tell you what to say. And I will send your brother Aaron with you. He shall speak for you when you need him."

And then God gave him a rod, or a staff, which he told Moses would work miracles and be of help in convincing the Hebrews that he had been sent by the Lord.

So Moses traveled back to Egypt. The Hebrews were anxious and excited when they heard that Moses had come back with a message from God. These people were a hardhearted bunch who had almost forgotten God's promise. They thought of it—when they did think of it—as an old tale told by their grandmothers. They weren't quite sure of Moses, who after all, had once been an Egyptian.

"Look at my rod," he commanded. With everyone's eyes upon him, he threw the rod down and it turned into a serpent at his feet. It slithered about, in and out of the screaming crowd, until Moses picked it up and it became a rod again.

The Hebrews were impressed. They bowed down and prayed to their God, thanking him for sending Moses.

Then Moses and Aaron went to the Pharaoh to ask for the release of the Hebrews. Aaron began, "The Lord of Israel says, 'Let my people go, that they may hold a feast for me in the wilderness.' "

Pharaoh sneered, "Who is your God, that I should obey his voice and let them go?" And he gave orders to work the Hebrews even harder.

"What should I do, Lord?" asked Moses.

"Use your rod," came the answer.

So the two brothers went to the Pharaoh again, and to show how mighty was their God, Moses threw his rod down. Once again it turned into a snake. It curled up around the Pharaoh's feet. But he just stepped aside and laughed.

"Hah, that is nothing," he sneered again. "My magicians have magic rods, too, and theirs are bigger and better." He clapped his hands and his magicians hurried out and threw their rods down and the ground was crawling with snakes.

Moses' snake grew larger and larger and swallowed up every single one of the Pharaoh's. The magicians were horrified and left in a flurry of silk capes.

"That doesn't mean anything," said the Pharaoh. "The Hebrews still stay."

Moses warned the king, "You had better listen, Pharaoh, or God will send plagues down upon you that are too awful to imagine. Let his people go!"

The Pharaoh just shook his head no. Moses went to the edge of the Nile and stretched forth his rod over the water. Immediately the river ran red. The water had turned into blood. Not only the river but also every jar of water, every rain barrel, every kettle of tea water on the fire—the water in every container turned to blood. Fish died and everything smelled awful.

Still the Pharaoh shook his head stubbornly. "*No!*"

At that moment, he heard the croaking of frogs. It grew so loud it sounded as if a million giants were hiccoughing. And then the frogs came and overran Egypt. Big ones, little ones, everywhere—in ovens and sweater drawers, under the sheets, inside boots and cookie

jars. *Everywhere.* When the Pharaoh sat down, he could feel them wiggling under him.

"All right," he called to Moses, "tell your God to take away the frogs and I will let your people go to make their sacrifice to him."

So Moses prayed the frogs away, and right then they died. Soon there were piles of them swept up everywhere, and their smell, combined with that of the blood, hung about every home, even the palace.

But when the Pharaoh saw the frogs were gone, he said, "Moses, I changed my mind. You can't go!"

"Very well," said Moses, and waited. Soon a black curtain of buzzing flies covered the land. They bit and stung and left large red hard spots on the Egyptians' bodies. Can you imagine working and sweating under that hot, hot sun, trying to brush off the flies in your eyes and nose and ears and between your shoulder blades where you can't reach?

The Pharaoh slapped his ear to stop the buzzing inside it and groaned, "Why can't you sacrifice right here in Egypt? That way I wouldn't have to worry about you coming back. Oh, all right, go on."

So the flies flew off, and as soon as he cleaned the last one out from between his toes, the Pharaoh snapped, "I didn't mean it, Moses, you stay!"

And Moses said, again, "Very well." That very day another plague came to Egypt. All the animals—the sheep and oxen and camels—began to get large ugly boils and many of them just lay down and died from them. Although he was very angry, the Pharaoh said he didn't care, the answer was still no.

On the next day it hailed huge hard baseballs of ice, which knocked down every palm tree, cornstalk, pumpkin and barley plant in Egypt. It thundered so loud the children would not come out from under their beds. Again the Pharaoh begged Moses to stop it, and when he did, the king hardened his heart and said the Hebrews could not leave.

A plague of locusts came next, swarms of buzzing, flying crawling insects which ate whatever the hail had left. They stuck to people's hair and the walls of their houses. Then came three days of complete darkness. And finally, the last and worst plague descended on Egypt.

"At midnight," Moses warned the Pharaoh, "God will send his angel of death across the land and the firstborn shall die, from the firstborn of the Pharaoh to that of his maidservant, and even the firstborn of the animals. But not all—you shall see how God has marked a difference between the Egyptians and the Israelites."

Moses commanded his people to prepare a meal of a lamb roasted whole and bread made without yeast. The fathers were to take a bunch of herbs which had been dipped in the blood of the lamb and make marks on the doorways of each home. As night fell the Hebrews went inside, locked the doors, and ate their last meal standing up, already dressed for a journey.

At midnight it happened as God had said. A shadow fell over Egypt as the angel of death approached. The angel passed over the Hebrew homes marked by the lambs' blood, but every firstborn child and animal of the Egyptians died. The Pharaoh's son was among them. The hardness of the king's heart finally cracked with grief.

He called Moses and, with great anger and sorrow, told him, "All of you, rise up and get out from among my people. You and your children of Israel, go and serve your God. Take your flocks and herds and be gone!"

The Egyptians wanted them out of the country as soon as possible for fear more plagues and sadness would come to them. "Hurry," they said, "lest we all be dead men."

Moses urged his people to hurry, too, for he was afraid the Pharaoh would change his mind again. There was a great noise and clatter and rush as people grabbed their belongings and joined the long line winding for miles out of Egypt. Chickens and goats and children plucked out of their beds, apple rings and mushrooms drying on strings—they were all part of the caravan leaving Egypt forever.

To give them courage, God went before them as a pillar of cloud by day and a pillar of fire by night. By morning they had reached the Red Sea, and the Hebrews pitched their tents along its shore.

Now, just as you'd think, the Pharaoh changed his mind *again*. He thought about losing all those workers. Who would build his granaries and cities and statues? He muttered to himself, "Why have I done this foolish thing? Why on earth did I let those people go?"

He called his army together, and with 600 chariots they set off to capture the Hebrews. Without much trouble, they began to catch up to them. When the Hebrews heard the thunder of 600 horses' hooves coming nearer and nearer, what do you think they did? Prayed to God? Trusted in God? Remained calm, knowing God would save them?

No! They acted like spoiled, spiteful children. They yelled at Moses and blamed him.

"Why have you done this to us? Why have you taken us out of Egypt to die in this wilderness? Didn't we tell you to let us alone to serve the Egyptians? We'd be better off to die there than here!"

Moses tried to answer them patiently: "Don't worry, my children. Stand still and see the salvation of God which he will show you this day. God shall fight for you, and you must hold your peace."

Then the pillar of cloud went behind them and got between the Hebrews and the galloping Egyptians. It gave light to the Hebrews but became a black shield against their pursuers, who could see nothing past it.

Then God told Moses to wave his rod over the stormy waters of the sea. The wind immediately changed to a gentle east breeze and the waters parted in the middle to make the dry sea bottom a path with waves on either side. Quickly, Moses gave the command to march forward. For a change the people didn't argue, and every single Hebrew, with animals and carts and bundles, got across safely.

Moses looked behind him and could see and smell the dust of chariots and the cries of the Egyptians. They had reached the shore and were plunging ahead on the dry sea bottom to catch up with the fleeing crowd.

"Dear Lord," cried Moses, "what now?"

The wind shifted as suddenly as it had before the sea parted.

It gusted violently and the open ground was covered with 10-foot waves. Because they couldn't stop, the chariots plowed straight ahead into the angry foaming water. On the opposite shore the Hebrews stood by speechless as the Egyptians, with their 600 chariots, and their Pharaoh, were swallowed up into the depths of the sea. Not one survived.

Thanks to Moses, the Hebrews were on their way to Canaan, the Promised Land. You'd think he would have been cheered and respected as their leader. He had truly set them free. If he were living today, there would probably be statues and parks and hospitals named after him. But he was not appreciated by his own people.

They grumbled, they complained, they were ungrateful, they were never satisfied. They acted the way some children do when their mothers make a batch of molasses cookies. The children throw them down and say, "I don't want those old things. I want chocolate with vanilla filling!"

Moses had to put up with them for 40 years, until they finally reached that beautiful land flowing with milk and honey. By then, God had given Moses two stone tablets with the laws to govern the tribes of Israel in all their acts. These laws, which we know as the Ten Commandments, would be the Word of God to the Hebrews until Jesus came and shared his new words with us.

Moses was in all ways a mighty man. He spent his life as a leader, prophet, law-giver. He was also the Hebrews' scapegoat. (A scapegoat is one who bears the blame for others.) When things went wrong, they *always* blamed Moses; when things went right, they forgot about him.

But Moses never lost sight of what he had been given to do. He obeyed God, even though he had to go to him as each problem tumbled over the other and ask, "What should I do now, Lord?"

Moses, unlike the spoiled children of Israel, praised and blessed God every inch of the desert road to Canaan. His God, he sang, "is merciful and gracious, long-suffering, and abundant in goodness and truth."

So was God's prophet, Moses.

137

The Woman at the Well

ong ago, there was a woman who became our Lord's first missionary because she couldn't keep a secret. She didn't just let it slip out accidentally and then try to cover it up. She untied it and let it loose, like a ball of yarn bouncing and unrolling down the stairs.

She ran up hills and down, across town and back, bursting through the doors of the grocery and bakery and chickenfeed stores, grabbing everyone who would listen—and some who wouldn't—to hear her incredible, out-of-this-world story. "Listen to me, you won't believe who I met today!" But by the time she was through, they *did* believe.

Her story began about noontime of that very day, a very hot summer's day. Our Lord had been traveling from Judea through Samaria, a country which most Jews despised. (The worst thing any Jew could call another in the heat of an argument was "You *Samaritan!*") But Jesus knew that *every* country had people who were waiting for him, and he knew that he would be meeting just such a one this very day.

He came to the small town of Sichar at midday. Very weary and dusty, he sat down in the shade beside a well. He was thinking how good a drink of that pure cold water would feel on his dry lips and throat when he saw a pleasant-looking, plump woman coming up the road. She carried a water jug gracefully on her hip.

The woman saw our Lord sitting there, but since he was not

one of her people, she looked away. He must be a Jew, she thought, and if so, he wouldn't speak to her anyway.

"Would you kindly give me a drink?" asked our Lord politely.

The woman, whose name might have been Clara, waited a moment before answering. Well, she decided, the poor man is thirsty, Jew or not. It can't hurt to give him some water.

Being curious, she asked him, "How is it that you, who must be a Jew, ask me, a Samaritan woman, for a drink? I thought you people wouldn't have anything to do with us." She sounded a bit snippy.

Jesus, who knew that this meeting would change Clara's life, answered in a way that puzzled her. "If you knew the gift of God and who is asking you for a drink, you perhaps would have asked him and he would have given you living water."

Now Clara could make neither head nor tail out of this. Whatever was the man talking about? What did he mean by *living* water? It could mean that he didn't think much of *their* well, which had been given to them by Jacob himself, long, long ago. That certainly wouldn't be very polite of him.

"Do you think you are greater than our ancestor Jacob, who gave us the well and drank from it himself?" she asked. And then, being a practical woman, she added, "Sir, from where do you get this living water? And what do you mean by that? Besides, you have nothing to draw the water with." While she talked, she had filled a ladle with water from her jug and offered it to Jesus.

He accepted it gratefully and said, "That was so good. But everyone who drinks of this water will become thirsty again. Whoever drinks of the water that I give shall never thirst, ever again. The water I give shall become a fountain inside, springing up into life everlasting."

Clara was completely befuddled by now. And yet, for some reason she could not understand, something was churning up inside her, as if there were indeed a fountain within that surged up like a geyser and went *whoooosh*! Every part of her began to tingle with prickles of excitement. She knew no ordinary man would promise her she would never thirst again. What a lot of time she would save if she didn't have to draw water every day!

Jesus went on. He knew there was much in her life that needed more than refreshment. "Go call your husband, and come back here," he told her quietly.

Clara hung her head. "I have no husband." She didn't want to say more, and there was no need to. Our Lord already knew the secrets of her life before he met her. He knew she had not obeyed the laws of marriage in the past or at this moment.

He did not waggle his finger at her, telling her she ought to be ashamed. He knew she was. Jesus just nodded and said, "You have said it well, 'I have no husband,' for I know you have had five husbands, and the man you are with now is not your husband. You have said it truly."

Clara was shaken. She had not understood our Lord's first words to her, but she certainly did these. How could this stranger whom she had never seen before know she had had five husbands, unless—

"Sir," she said, kneeling down quickly at his feet, "I think that you are a prophet." She wanted very much to talk of something else. What did it matter to this man how she spent her life?

"And since you are a prophet," she went on, "perhaps you can tell me where is the right place to worship? Our people say it is on this mountain. You Jews say it is in Jerusalem. Who is right?"

He answered her, "The hour is coming—it is now here— when the true worshipers will worship the Father in spirit and in truth."

Impossible ideas were filling Clara's head. She had heard exciting rumors whenever the men of the village gathered together to talk. Looking right into Jesus' eyes, she said, "I know that the Messiah is coming, whom we call Christ, and I know that he will tell us all things."

And then Jesus said, as in her heart she had dared to hope he would, "I am he, speaking with you!"

These words set off the geyser of living water inside Clara. She exploded and bubbled joy all over the place and could not keep still.

This was too much for her to keep as a secret; she must share this marvelous news with every person in town. She left her water jug with Jesus and ran, in a great, zigzagging hurry, back down the road to town.

She called out to anyone who would stop, and she talked as fast as her tongue could go without tripping. "Listen, this is the absolute truth. I met a man who told me all that I have ever done. Is he not the Christ?" Over and over again she told her story and asked this question. Some of the women turned away and sniffed.

"Of course he knows about Clara. Who in Sichar *doesn't* know about her?" they said nastily.

But some people sat quietly and listened and then followed her back to meet this man. When Jesus spoke to them, they too believed as Clara did and wanted to become his followers right then and there. They begged our Lord to stay with them and teach for a few days, and he did.

Then they went back to their village and shared the news with their spouses, and they went out and told their neighbors, who went shopping the next day and told the butcher and the plumber and the man who cleans chimneys. And he went out and told his cousins in another town who were working in a vineyard, and they told some mushroom-pickers who were passing by on their way to the woods, and they told a group of bird-watchers in the woods, who became so excited you'd have thought they had found a yellow-bellied sapsucker!

Before long, all of Samaria was talking about the stranger at Jacob's well and about his promise, and all because our Lord asked the woman for a drink of water.

There's a joke so old it probably was around in Jesus' time. It goes:

What is the fastest way for news to spread?
Telephone? No.
Telegram? No.
Tell-a-woman? Yes!

I wonder if it crossed our Lord's mind as he watched Clara come up the road!

The Man Born Blind

here was once a man who knew no difference between the rising of the moon and the setting of the sun. Dawn or dusk, it was all the same to him because he had been born blind. He never knew colors or books or the face of his mother and, although he could feel or smell them, he had never seen an apple pie or brussels sprouts or the insides of a milkweed pod.

He would shrug his shoulders and say, "If you don't know what you're missing, then you don't miss it," and then add, "...*much*," under his breath. He tried to get through each day without causing anyone too much trouble or bumping into a camel while crossing the street. Sometimes he did step on somebody's wash drying on the rocks, but because he was blind, no one really got angry with him.

He spent his days sitting at the edge of the road in a busy spot, begging. One Sunday, as he sat wondering if the wind in the trees had a color, he heard a group of people coming towards him. "As long as I am in the world, I must do the work of him who sent me, for I am the light of the world," someone was saying.

This someone stopped in front of where the blind man was sitting and, without any explanation, mixed some dirt from the ground with spit until it was thick as mud and spread it upon the beggar's eyes. "Now," he said to the man, "go and wash in the pool of Siloam."

Imagine how the blind man felt! He was quite startled when

144

Jesus—for that's who it was—began to put the mud on his eyes, and a bit afraid because he was helpless to stop him. But there was something in Jesus' touch and in his voice that lifted the fear. He picked himself up and began to walk to the pool, followed by a group of curious villagers.

When he came to it, he did as Jesus had told him. He washed away the mud. For the first time ever, he saw the clear rippling of water. Then he blinked his eyes, and there, reflected in that water, was a face. So that's what a nose and mouth and eyes looked like! He smiled at the face, and it smiled back. It was *his* face! He rejoiced, because he certainly was much better-looking than ever he had imagined.

He stumbled up the bank and ran and danced along the road, calling to his friends and neighbors. They exclaimed, "Will you look at that! Why, isn't that Harold, who was born blind and who sits and begs by the side of the road?"

"Yes!" He smiled so broadly his eyes almost closed again. "I am Harold!"

(I'm not sure his name was Harold, but it *could* have been Harold. It is much nicer to call someone by name rather than just "the blind man.")

He told them what had happened and how Jesus had told him to go and wash in the pool at Siloam. "And I went and I washed," he said, "and now I see."

The people murmured and said he must go to the Pharisees, a group of religious leaders who often thought they were much holier than anyone else, and ask them the meaning of his cure. This was beyond their understanding.

So Harold went to the Pharisees, certain they would be as joyous as he over his good fortune. He explained once more the miracle which Jesus had worked, and the Pharisees listened quietly. They said nothing out loud, but in their hearts, they were frightened. They had already heard of Jesus and were afraid that his message would shake up their comfortable lives.

Some of them said, "This Jesus is not of God because he performed a miracle on the Sabbath, which is a holy day." Others said,

"How can a man who is not of God work such a miracle in the first place?"

So they asked Harold what *he* thought. Up to that moment,

he hadn't thought very much about Jesus or God or religion at all. He had lived in his dark, unchanging world with his thoughts and a bit of food and talk by the roadside, knowing that time had passed only when the noonday sun warmed the morning chill from his bones.

Now, everything was changed because of this Jesus. He saw all those things which had been only words to him before. He saw the shades of blue in the deep August sky, the chicory by the road, his mother's eyes. And tomorrow he would see the day dawn for the first time.

He told the Pharisees boldly, "He is a prophet."

But the Pharisees would not believe this. They went to his parents, who were a bit nervous about attracting attention, and asked them sternly, "Is this your son who was born blind? Then how do you say he can see now?"

They answered honestly, "We know nothing of this. All we know is that this morning Harold was blind, and now he sees. Who did this, we don't know. Why don't you ask Harold? He's old enough to speak for himself."

The Pharisees insisted. "Are you sure, absolutely, definitely, without question, that your son was born blind?"

The mother answered sharply, becoming less nervous, "Of course I'm *absolutely* sure. After all, I was there, you know." And his father added, "Of course, definitely, no doubt about it."

The Pharisees returned to question Harold, who had been blowing bubbles from a clay pipe and watching them soar as round patches of rainbows into the sun. "Harold," they said, "we want you to think carefully and tell us the truth. We know this man is a sinner."

Harold answered quickly, more boldly than before. "I don't know if he is a sinner. All I know is that I was blind and now I see." He was beginning to wonder about this Jesus, about whom he knew almost nothing.

The Pharisees asked again how Jesus had cured him. Harold was beginning to lose his patience but he held his tongue and repeated, step by step, the story of Jesus and the mud and the pool. "I have told you this already and then once again. Why are you so interested in what I say? Do *you* want to become disciples?"

At this, the Pharisees became enraged. "What? Why, we are the disciples of Moses. We know that God spoke to Moses, but what do we know of this imposter? Disciples, indeed!"

Harold was so sure Jesus could not be a sinner that he said fearlessly, "A wonderful thing has happened here. This man has opened my eyes and you do not know where he is from. We know—even *I* know—that God doesn't hear sinners. But if anyone loves him and does his will, then God listens to him. No one has ever heard that a man could open the eyes of one born blind. If Jesus didn't come from God, he couldn't do this. He couldn't do anything."

This angered the Pharisees further. How dare this nothing-of-a-beggar explain away his miracle so clearly and reasonably!

"How dare *you,* who were born in sin, teach *us!*" they shouted at him as they cast him out of the town. He was alone and not quite as fearless as nightfall wrapped him in its darkness.

Jesus heard what had happened and went to search for Harold. He found him crouched against the village wall. He put his arm around him, and Harold felt his love and concern and stopped shivering.

"Do you believe in the Son of God?" asked Jesus. Harold answered, "Who is he, Lord, that I might believe in him?"

And Jesus said, "You have seen him, and it is he who is talking with you!"

At that moment, Harold saw Jesus not as an unknown stranger who had healed his blindness, nor as a prophet who angered the Jews, but as his Creator. His heart as well as his eyes opened to the Light.

It is said that from that time on he was a disciple of Christ and, much later on, a bishop by the name of Restitus. I suppose this would be a very good name for him, since the word *restitution* means a putting back or restoring something to the way it ought to be.

But I like Harold better.

148

Veronica

ccording to an old Christian legend, a very kind and brave woman became a saint by wiping the face of a weary man. Her name was Veronica and the face was that of Jesus. She was in the crowd which gathered to watch our Lord stagger and fall as he carried his cross up the hill to Calvary. But she didn't just stop to look. She stepped out of the crowd and will be known forever for one brief, brave act of caring.

The heavy wooden beams of the cross pressed down on Jesus' shoulders with every step he took. Blood from the thorn-crown jammed into his head trickled down his cheeks and mixed with the sweat of his struggle to climb the hill. The burning sun made him long for the days he had spent teaching by the sea. A sudden wind stirred up the dust of the road and blew it into his face so he could not see. He stumbled upon a sharp rock and fell, the cross on top of him.

Veronica watched all this until she could stand it no longer. She was not a follower of Jesus, or even one of his own people. She was the wife of a Roman general, probably on her way to the Temple of Beauty for a massage when she was caught up by this mob, so noisily eager for the crucifixion.

When she saw this man, an ordinary criminal for all she knew, straining with unsure feet towards the spot where he would die, something happened in her tender heart. She stepped out and knelt

beside the fallen man. She unwrapped the white linen veil from her head and gently pressed it to his face. The blood, sweat and grime soaked into the cloth. She lifted it away carefully so it would not stick. Jesus gazed at her with a look of love she would never forget. She sat there, the cloth in her hand, unable to move.

Then the rough voices of the soldiers shouting, "Move on. Move on. Out of the way. Let's have order here!" jolted her. She remembered where she was and who she was and disappeared into the crowd, the cloth hidden under her robe.

That evening, she decided to get rid of the veil and put the puzzling happening out of her mind. The veil dropped open to the floor as she unfolded it, and on it Veronica saw, the legend insists, the *veronicon,* the "true image" of Jesus. His face was printed on the cloth just as it had been when she soothed Jesus along his Way of the Cross—the thorned crown, the tear-shaped drops of blood, the loving look.

After many centuries people brought what they believed to be Veronica's veil to Rome, where it remains to this day.

We don't know much more about Veronica. We wonder if her husband found out and was angry with her, or if he didn't care. Perhaps God lifted the veil from the eyes of her soul so she could see that Jesus was really the Son of God. All we know is that she cared enough about another person's pain to forget about herself. In that one moment, she answered Christ's call to "Come, follow me."

When you wipe the toast crumbs or milk-mustache from the mouth of one too weak to do it himself, or dry the dishes for a mother with very tired feet, or polish the windows of an elderly neighbor so the sunlight may come through and warm her bones, then you too are a *Veronica,* a true image of our Lord.

Simon of Cyrene

nce there was a man called who carried the cross for Jesus. Sometimes you may hear people speak of carrying *their* crosses, and this usually means putting up with prickly problems and people and not making a fuss about them. A cross could be anything from having a nosy neighbor who listens in on your telephone calls to spending your life in a wheelchair, being shy, having a stutter, or not having a father. Lots of people (all of us) carry their own crosses, sometimes not too happily.

But Simon carried the first *real* cross, the one on which Jesus was nailed. And Simon was no more willing to accept that burden than we are today. Our crosses are like toothpicks compared to that thick beam of wood eight feet long.

When Simon left his home in the country for Jerusalem that Friday morning, he had no idea that he would be one of the last persons to give comfort to Jesus on earth. He may not even have known of Jesus. He came from Cyrene, a town on the coast of Africa, and could have been a Jew or a Gentile or a black African. All we know is that the Gospel calls him a "stranger."

As he walked through Jerusalem that day, Simon suddenly found himself in the midst of a crowd. Everyone was shouting and jeering at a man staggering under the weight of a cross as a group of soldiers led him up the street. Simon stood still, wondering what was going on, until one of the soldiers singled him out and said, "That one looks good and strong, get him!"

The soldiers told Simon to help the weakened prisoner carry his cross. This was not because they suddenly felt pity for Jesus but because they were afraid he might die before he got to the top of Calv-

ary. Then they wouldn't have their execution and the mob would be angry.

So, the Gospel says, they *forced* Simon to take up the cross. Now anyone who is forced to do something doesn't want to do it. Simon was disgusted with the dirt and the smell and the blood and the weeping of women and the hoarse meanness of the crowd. To be forced to have any part of it made him ashamed.

Yet he must have feared the soldiers because he did not refuse. He probably thought he might as well just do it and get it over with and then get on with his own business in town. Maybe he was a rug merchant or camel-trader. Whatever he was, he was not a man who wanted to carry someone's cross.

He ignored our Lord, as if it were his fault. He swung the beam's end upon his shoulders and walked behind Jesus, trying not to step on his feet.

Our Lord knew how he felt, of course. "I am sorry to be so slow, my friend, and I'm very sorry that you must be here. I do not wish anyone to bear my cross unwillingly," he spoke quietly.

Simon said nothing but took more of the cross upon his back until he carried it all. Jesus was growing too weak to walk under its weight, but for some reason it seemed lighter to Simon than when he first lifted it to his shoulders.

Before they reached the hilltop, Simon's heart had been touched by God's grace, and he knew that Jesus was truly the King of the Jews. After our Lord's death, Simon became one of his disciples and his two sons, Alexander and Rufus, followed Jesus as well. They traveled with zeal and love to spread Christ's Good News, and it is said that all three of them became bishops in Spain.

Simon must have wondered if Jesus had him in mind when, in a happier time, he taught another crowd on another mountain:

"Whoever forces you to go for one mile,
Go with him two . . . ."

Simon went with Jesus two and three and all the rest of the miles it took to fill up his earthly lifetime.

Dismas

 any years ago, there was a thief who stole everything he could get his hands on. He stole rubber bands and Hershey bars and tulip bulbs and doghouses. He grabbed clean underwear from Monday washlines and hot pretzels with mustard from pushcarts. In the still of the night, he beat the robber raccoons to the just-ripe corn. Once he stole a bushel of parsnips but returned it when he tasted one. Once he stole a camel. And once, just once, he stole heaven.

But that is beginning at the end. His story begins the night the Holy Family was warned by an angel to flee to Egypt because Herod was about to kill all the baby boys in Bethlehem. The angel left no doubt that they were to go *now,* so quickly and sleepily, Mary gathered up Jesus, and Joseph packed a goat-skin filled with water, some fig bars and fresh diapers into a basket.

Joseph put Mary and the baby Jesus and the basket on their donkey and they set off on the four-day journey to Egypt. On the second day, when they were quite tired and hot and the water was almost gone, they came to a bunch of palm trees and sighed with relief. Now they could rest in the shade and find more water.

But no sooner had they begun to unpack the basket than two wild-eyed young robbers jumped out from behind the trees. One, named Gestas, was all for taking everything, including the donkey, and leaving the family there to die. After all, who would know and who would care?

155

It was just one family.

But the other, a young man named Dismas who was just starting out as a thief, looked into the clear eyes of the young mother and turned away.

"Aw, let them go." He shrugged his shoulders as if he didn't care. "What've they got anyway? Nothing worthwhile, just a bunch of fig bars. And what would *we* do with diapers?"

Gestas grabbed the fig bars and began to shove them into his mouth as if he hadn't eaten for weeks. (Actually, it had been about three days.) "Here, take them all, you must be hungry," said Mary politely. She didn't want him to feel bad because he had grabbed them from her.

"What kind of robber are you?" Gestas asked Dismas with scorn. "There probably won't be anybody coming by here again for weeks. And last time, *you* got all the good stuff—the gold watch and the licorice strings. All I got was the flyswatter and a pen that didn't work. I say we take everything and forget about them."

Dismas looked at the child sleeping in Mary's arms. "Suppose I give you 40 pieces of gold and a pen that does write and we let them go."

Gestas raised his eyebrows and said, "Well, now, that's different. Goodbye, folks, you'd better get on your way. Nothing personal, but a fellow has to make a living, you know."

Before he returned to the hiding-place beneath the palm trees, Dismas filled the goatskin with fresh water for the family's trip. Mary thanked him. "May God be merciful to you and forgive you your sins on Judgement Day!" she said. Dismas did not answer. He didn't like to think of such things.

Dismas and Gestas continued to steal and squabble over who should get what. And so they spent their lives—running, hiding, robbing and maybe even murdering. They were outcasts from all that was comfortable and respectable. At last they were caught and condemned to die. A fitting end to such scoundrels, everyone agreed. They were as useless as yesterday's garbage, unwanted and unpleasant to have around. Good riddance!

All those years, Jesus had been growing up and preparing for his life of teaching and healing and loving. At last the day came, as he knew it must, when he would show how much he loved us by dying on the cross.

Now it is just as easy to crucify three criminals as one, and so Dismas and Gestas were led out to Calvary with Jesus and nailed to crosses on either side of him.

There they were, hanging in the air beside a foolish man who thought himself the King of the Jews. What a joke! If they were not in such pain, they might have joined the yelling of the mob:"Look at him! He saved others; himself he cannot save! He trusted in God, let God deliver him now if he will have him!"

Gestas, his heart full of hurt and hate, cried out, "If you are Christ, then save yourself—and us too!"

But Dismas gasped, "Have you no fear of God, Gestas? We are getting no more than what we deserve, the reward of our deeds. But this man has done nothing wrong."

With an effort, Dismas raised his eyes to our Lord. There was something about this man, and that woman with the sad white face standing at the foot of the cross. Had he ever met them? More likely, he thought, he had robbed them. He felt a great stab of sorrow for all the selfish things he had done, taking money and food and animals from people who needed them. He wished he could begin all over again.

"Lord," he whispered to Jesus, "remember me when you come into your Kingdom!"

Jesus' heart was touched, for was not this the very reason he had come to earth, to save souls?

"Dismas," he said, "I promise you, this day you shall be with me in paradise!"

And so the last person Jesus met on his earthly journey was the first to travel with him on his way back home. At the final moment, Dismas stole heaven. He was a *very* good thief, indeed!

As for Gestas, we know nothing more. Perhaps, before his very last breath, he realized there was one thing he couldn't steal and didn't have to—Jesus' love for every one of us. All he had to do was believe in it. And let us hope that he did.

John Bread·and·Water

here once was a saint
Who won holy fame
As Blessed John Bread-and-Water
(Since he lived in Spain
He went by the name
Of *Juan pan-y-agua*)

And what did he do,
This little brother?
He lived his life through
On just bread and water.

No butter or jam
To spread on each slab,
No chicken or ham
Or picked meat of crab,

No lemon curd custard
Went onto his bread,
Or sardines in mustard,
Or pimiento cheese spread.

He never knew cream cheese
With olives or dates,
He just smiled and ate
The crumbs on his plate.

And what of the crusts
That sat on his platter?
Whether buckwheat or bran,
It just didn't matter.
  (Of one thing we are sure,
  It was the bread *du jour*.)

And what else did he do,
Brother John of Navarre?
Did he cobble shoes?
Examine a star?

Did he ring the bells?
Or pot the chives?
Or polish shells?
Or dust archives?

He probably did, all this and much more,
Without any fuss or hint of hauteur,
But just as a plus, for the love of our Lord,
He ate only bread, he drank only water.

And that is why, in a tiny note
In a musty book,
You read of John, who is only known
For what he forsook.

Peter

nce upon a time, there was a fisherman named Simon who was quite satisfied with his way of life. He had never gone to school and wasn't interested in reading poetry or discussing the Law or arguing over how to worship God. He was a simple man who was concerned with what he could see and touch and smell—like fish.

Simon was sturdily built, with dark curly hair and beard. His skin was browned and toughened from the beating of sun and wind upon it, for he spent from morning to dusk by the sea at Galilee. With his brother Andrew, he was either mending his nets or pulling them, fat and full with fish, over the side of his boat. Simon asked no more than this for contentment.

One day a stranger came by and stopped to watch them unloading the day's catch. The stranger looked into Simon's eyes, and Simon felt as if his soul had been caught in a net too.

"Come, follow me," said the stranger, who was Jesus.

And Simon and Andrew, without a word, did just that.

"Today you catch fish," said Jesus, "but from now on, you shall be fishers of men." The brothers did not understand this at first, but in the days and weeks ahead they discovered who Jesus was and why he was here. Then they lost no time in casting their nets to catch the souls who hungered for Christ's message.

Simon was the first to say to Jesus' face, "I know you are the Christ, the Son of the living God" when the others were afraid to say so out loud. Our Lord knew he was going to be the leader of the apostles when he was gone, so he said to him, "Simon, from now on you shall be called Cephas" (which was the word for *rock* in their language and which is *Peter* in ours).

Jesus went on to say, "Blessed are you, Peter, because no one has told you who I am but my Father who is in heaven. You are the rock on which I will build my Church, and the powers of hell shall not prevail against it. I will give you the keys of the Kingdom of Heaven, and whatever you bind on earth shall be bound in heaven; whatever you loose on earth, it shall be loosed also in heaven."

Peter seemed a good choice to be the leader of the apostles. He was always the first to jump up and agree, "You're right, Lord!" Or, "I'll do it, Lord!" Or, "You can count on me, Lord!" He was an eager beaver; he just couldn't wait to show Jesus how much he loved him. "Anything, Lord, anything; you just name it and I'll do it!"

But Peter didn't always act as he talked. He truly loved our Lord, and when he said he would die for him, he meant it—when he said it. Peter's problem was that he always stopped to think—and then to doubt, and then to worry. When he was busy worrying, he didn't have the faith to be brave.

Once when Jesus went up to the moutains to pray, the disciples got into their boat to go home across the Sea of Galilee. When they were almost halfway across, the sky suddenly grew dark and full of angry fuzzy black clouds. A squall came up that tossed their boat about from wave to wave. The disciples were terribly frightened, Peter most of all.

Then Andrew nudged Peter, "Look," he said, "there's Jesus!" And sure enough, there was our Lord, walking on top of the water with his hands outstretched toward them. Peter spoke first with a rush of brave words, "Lord, if it is you, bid me to come to you over the water."

Jesus answered, "You're right, Peter, it is I. Don't be afraid, come across the water to me."

So Peter reached out and took a step over the side of the boat onto the water. At the same time, he began to think, "What am I doing? This is absolutely crazy. *No one* can walk on water. I shall drown!" And he began to sink. He called out to Jesus, "Lord, save me!"

Of course Jesus grabbed his hand and did save him, but not without making him feel a little ashamed. Our Lord said gently, "Oh you of little faith. Why did you doubt, Peter?"

In spite of his weakness, Peter was still the most favored among the disciples. For the next two years, he followed Jesus into every town and home and marketplace, listening to him teach, questioning, learning and preparing for that time when Jesus said he would no longer be with them. He went everywhere with Jesus and saw the miracles of healing which, our Lord promised, "He that believes in me and the works that I do shall also do."

The night before Jesus was to die on the cross, Jesus gathered his friends together for one last meal and told them his time on earth was drawing to an end.

"Lord," asked Peter, "where are you going?"

"I am going where you can't follow me now, but you shall come after me later on."

"Why not?" impatient Peter cried. "Lord, why can't I follow you *now*? I am ready to lay down my life for your sake."

"Are you really, Peter?" smiled our Lord, sadly. "I know that before the rooster crows tomorrow morning, you will deny me three times." Peter could not find the words to answer. He was deeply hurt that Jesus would think such a thing.

Later that night, when Jesus was praying after supper in the Garden of Gethsemane, the soldiers came to find him and bring him to trial before the authorities. Peter watched from the shadows and followed them. He found a bush big enough to hide him and scrunched down to listen. His heart ached to see Jesus standing there, his hands and feet bound by rope.

A girl who had once brought the disciples some wine came

over to Peter and stared at him closely.

"Don't I know you?" she asked, squinting at him. "Aren't you one of those fellows who followed Jesus around?"

"Who me?" gasped Peter, appearing to be shocked. "I don't know what you're talking about. Who is Jesus?"

She called her girlfriend over and they whispered. The girlfriend said, "Yes, you are. You're a friend of Jesus. I've seen you with him!"

Peter snapped back, "You're crazy, I never saw the man before!"

A gardener who was trimming the thornapples nearby said, "You must be one of his followers or you wouldn't be so excited."

Then Peter began to yell and stamp his foot and shout bad things at the man, the way some people do when they are guilty but want to pretend they're not.

That moment a rooster crowed. Peter remembered what Jesus had said to him at supper, and he went away into the woods and cried his heart out. How could he ever face our Lord again? Would he ever have a chance now to say he was sorry?

To his joy, he did. The morning after Easter Sunday, our Lord appeared to the disciples, who had gone fishing to try to forget their sorrow. "Look," John said, "it is the Lord standing on the shore." Peter could not wait until they rowed ashore. He jumped into the water and swam so fast the fish got out of his way. He could think only that he had been given this chance to show Jesus how much he truly loved him.

Our Lord had a fire started on the shore and cooked them a breakfast of fresh-caught fried trout and crusty big rolls. What a beautiful meal it was, all of them together on the spot where they had been together so many times before. He comforted them and told them to be joyful for he would be with them through all the days to come until the end of the world.

And then he turned to Peter and showed how his love was stronger than Peter's weakness. Three times he asked his disciple, "Peter, do you love me?" And each time Peter said, "You know I do,

Lord,'' as if to make up for the three times he had denied Jesus before he died.

Twice after Peter answered him, our Lord said, "Feed my lambs," and the third time, "Feed my sheep." Peter understood then that he had been forgiven and was still to be the leader of the disciples. He knew that Christ, the Good Shepherd, had given his life for his flock, and that he, Peter, was to be their new shepherd on earth.

When the Holy Spirit came upon him on the first Pentecost, Peter was filled with such courage he knew that he would never again lie or be afraid. With all his doubts behind him, he set out to do the work

of the Lord. One day he and John went to the Temple to pray, and at the gate they met a poor man, lame since birth, who asked them for money. Peter stopped and said to him, "Look at us!" and the man did so eagerly. He hoped to see a coin in Peter's hand, for the only way he could buy food for himself was to beg.

But Peter said, "Silver and gold I do not have, but what I have I give you: In the name of Jesus Christ of Nazareth, arise and walk!" And taking the crippled man by the right hand, he lifted him up.

Timidly the man straightened himself, holding tight to Peter. He took one small shaky step, and then another and another until he was walking without any help. The man leaped into the air with joy and ran into the Temple to praise God.

For 25 years Peter traveled the world and taught about Jesus. He became the rock of strength all the new Christians and their communities needed.

Peter had become the Bishop of Rome when a new persecution broke out there against the Christians. The Emperor, Herod Agrippa, condemned Peter to death on the cross. Legend says both he and Paul went to heaven on the same day, on the same road outside the gates of Rome. It must have been *quite* a celebration when those two arrived in heaven together!

When our Lord said, "You are Peter, and upon this rock I will build my Church," he meant it in more ways than one. On the spot in Rome where Peter is buried is built the Church of St. Peter. In it is the throne, called the Chair of Peter, on which our Pope sits today.

Peter gives us the courage to keep on trying when we see how he picked himself up and started all over again. No matter how often we let our Lord down, we begin anew the moment we are sorry.

Once Peter asked Jesus how many times we should forgive someone. Seven times? Seventy times?

Jesus said, "How about 70 times seven?" He meant there is no end to forgiving.

Maybe he was smiling to himself, thinking of all the times he had to forgive Peter, who nevertheless stumbled straight into heaven.

Thomas

here was once a saint called Doubting Thomas who was very bothersome to live with because he was a skeptic. He was one of our Lord's 12 apostles, so you'd think he would know better than to be a skeptic. A skeptic, in case you might not know, is someone who doesn't believe anything you tell him unless he sees it for himself.

"Show me! Prove it!" Thomas would say with a cool eye and a bored look. "If I can't see it, touch it, smell it, I don't believe it."

If Peter would say, "Tomorrow should be a good day for fishing because the sunset today was a beautiful red—" (you know, "...red at night, sailor's delight"), Thomas would answer, "I don't know about that. It could just as easily rain."

Or, if Philip would bring in a nice warm egg, fresh from the hen, for breakfast, Thomas would look at it, feel it and shrug, "How do you know it is fresh? She could have been sitting on it for three days and that's why it's warm."

So you can see, Thomas could be a trial to the other apostles. But they loved him even during his worst questioning. They knew they also had faults which probably bothered him.

Thomas even questioned our Lord's rising from the tomb on the first Easter morning. The evening of that happy day, Jesus appeared to the apostles in their locked room (they were frightened because they

169

hadn't met the Holy Spirit yet), but Thomas was off on an errand.

They couldn't wait to tell Thomas. He listened to them with his cool manner and then sniffed, "I think you've been seeing things. There is no way I'll believe he was here. We've all been under a strain, you know—I think it's all wishful thinking."

A week later, Jesus appeared to them again, walking right through the door and up to Thomas. "I bring you my peace, Thomas," he said to his startled apostle. He showed his hands to him.

"Look, Thomas, do you see the scars from the nails? And give me your hand; put it in my side. Do you feel the wound and see the blood? Do you believe now, Doubting Thomas?"

Thomas could not look at our Lord. He hung his head and was very, very ashamed that he had so little faith. If he could believe that apple blossoms could turn into apples why could he not believe that Jesus could be standing here alive and well, sharing their meal?

He fell to Jesus' feet and covered his eyes. "My Lord and my God," he whispered, "I believe!"

Jesus smiled and said, "Now that you've seen me, Thomas, you believe. But how much more blessed are they who have not seen and yet believe. Think about that."

So Thomas thought about it and made up his mind from that moment on, he would not be a skeptic.

He no longer said "Show me!" or "Prove it!" If someone told him that eggplants in Mongolia grew in the shape of bananas, he would nod his head and reply, "That is very interesting, and I really would like to see one." This made life easier for everyone, including Thomas.

Now he had to use all his energy and wit for preaching to strangers instead of arguing with friends. After Pentecost, the apostles spread out to bring Christ's word to the rest of the world. Legend says that our Lord appeared to Thomas again and told him that he would like him to go to India, which was not one of Thomas's favorite places.

"Oh, Lord," he groaned, "send me anywhere else. Thuringia — Lapland — Northumbria — Westphalia — but not *India*!"

171

Jesus said, "India, Thomas. Don't worry, I will watch over you while you go tell everyone we are all brothers and sisters with one Father."

And Thomas remembered about believing without seeing, so he packed his bag for India.

After he got used to it, Thomas came to love his new home and the kind, loving people who lived in it and who soaked up God's word like sunshine. He could see how, as always, God's will was wiser than his own desire.

Thomas made such a name for himself he even impressed the king, whose name was Gundafor. One day Gundafor called Thomas to his palace and asked him what else he could do besides talk about this God the king didn't know.

"Well," said Thomas, "I can build houses and make plows and oars and shipmasts and carve tombs and . . ."

"That's enough," said the king. "I've been looking for the right person to build me a new palace. The one we have now is getting cramped and the children need more room. You'll have to make the swimming pool larger, and I'd like a few extra rooms for a bakery and a cheese house, a library with a stained-glass door, a rabbit hutch and a tree-house, of course. Well, here are the plans and some money for you to buy what you need."

Gundafor left Thomas with a huge bag of gold and told him he would be back in a few months after a trip to Persia. Thomas looked at all that money and thought of what Jesus said about laying up treasure in heaven instead of on earth. He decided to do a marvelous thing for the king: He gave all the money away to the poor, every bit of it.

When Gundafor returned, he went right to Thomas, saying, "I can't wait to see my new palace. I've been thinking of nothing else all the way home."

"Well, your Highness," said Thomas, taking a deep breath, "your palace is waiting for you but you can't see it now. Only when you have left this world."

"What! I can't see it *now*? Where is it?" asked the king, sounding annoyed.

"It's in heaven. I have laid up a treasure for you that will never rot or be destroyed by wind or rain or moths. I gave your money to your poor subjects in Christ's name. And now your mansion in heaven is beyond anything I could ever build. Stained-glass windows as well as doors . . ."

The king wanted his palace *now*. "Show me! Prove it!" he roared. Since Thomas couldn't do either, Gundafor cast him into prison. "Tomorrow you shall die for stealing my money. This is nothing but a Christian trick."

That night Gundafor's brother, who had recently died and gone to heaven, came back to earth to tell Gundafor about the beautiful palace awaiting him, with a bower of honeysuckle climbing up the stained-glass door and a goldfish pond in the back yard. "You can't believe how nice it is, my brother. Would you mind if I used it now since you don't need it yet?" And the brother vanished without waiting for an answer.

Gundafor was stunned and could say nothing. Then he realized what Thomas had been trying to tell him. Gundafor freed Thomas at once and asked him to baptize the entire royal family that very day.

He told Thomas how sorry he was for having doubted him, and Thomas just smiled and said not to worry about it. After all, who could understand better than one who once was known as Doubting Thomas?

Stephen

ot long after Jesus returned to heaven, there was a disciple called Stephen who became the first martyr, the first to die for Christ. He didn't intend to be, but it just worked out that way. He thought he would spend his life in Jerusalem, taking care of the poor and the sick and the widows and the orphans, for that was the job that had been given him by the apostles.

This time just after the Ascension of our Lord was very busy. There were just so many apostles and they had to scramble and scatter and scoot up and down the streets and they still could not get all the work done that Christ wanted them to do. Their most important jobs were to pray and heal, to teach and preach the Good News, but they also had to take care of the needy. Jesus had told them that whatever they did for the least of his brothers and sisters, they did for him too.

So they asked Stephen and six other men, all of whom the Bible says were "full of grace and fortitude," to be deacons, to take care of their needy brethren. It wasn't as exciting as traveling to pagan countries to live (and maybe die) for Christ, but this was where Stephen was needed.

Along with God's grace and strength, Stephen had been given a very large gift of humility. Instead of doing great things, he had been chosen to do many bite-size, stay-at-home jobs that wouldn't be much noticed except by our Lord. "Well," he said, "if that's the way you want it, Lord, I'm off and running! First, I'll need earmuffs for the orphans . . .''

And whatever else people needed—hot water bottles, firewood, turnip seeds—he made sure they got them. No matter how small the need or how boring (sometimes the older ladies liked to talk and talk and *talk*), he knew he was taking Christ's place. So he tried to be as interested and loving as he could.

Sometimes he did feel like grumbling, as when he had a week's worth of garbage to dump or when he poked a hole into a wasps' nest while painting the attic window, but he never let it show. As long as he was giving his life, he told himself, he was going to be cheerful about it.

This upset the religious leaders of the Jews, and the more good he did, the angrier they became. "This Christian must be dealt with," they told each other very seriously. *Dealt with,* to them, meant that they had to do away with the young trouble-maker.

Since they could find nothing wrong with Stephen's bringing milk and honey to hungry families, they paid some witnesses to lie about what he *said* in their homes. They dragged him off to the Temple to accuse him of offending God and Moses. Once they had listed all his crimes, they gave him permission to speak.

Stephen's face shone like that of an angel, radiant and surrounded by light. He told them that the laws given to Abraham and Moses were right and part of God's plan for preparing the world for Jesus, but they were enough only for those long-ago times. When Jesus came as the Son of God, he brought a new law.

Then he spoke more sharply and called the leaders stiff-necked and deaf to the Holy Spirit. He said that their fathers had persecuted the prophets before Christ, and that they themselves had betrayed Christ when he came!

Well, as you can imagine, this made Stephen's enemies furious. They shouted at him and put their hands over their ears so they would not hear such dreadful things. They hurled themselves upon him, knocked him down and dragged him out of the Temple and the city too.

They had decided to deal with this irritating Christian by stoning him to death.

They gathered all manner of rocks and small boulders from the roadside and walls and stream beds, and when they felt they had enough, they took off their shirts and coats so they wouldn't get mussed up or soiled. Then they asked a loud, fierce-eyed young member of the group called Saul if he would watch their clothes. He was glad to do it. Anything to help get rid of these ridiculous Christians!

As the rocks whizzed about him, Stephen must have felt a pang of sadness that he hadn't been able to do as much as he wanted in this life. But he still had the strength and love to call out, "Lord Jesus, receive my spirit. Do not lay this sin upon them!" Just as our Lord asked the Father to forgive his captors, so Stephen prayed for mercy for the angry stone-throwers.

When the crowd left, a few Christians took his body and buried it secretly. The next day a persecution broke out against all the believers and many went into hiding. The disciples left hurriedly for other lands and only the apostles stayed in Jerusalem.

Of all their enemies, the young man named Saul was the most determined to find and kill the Christians. He went from house to house, searching behind curtains and under beds and inside toy chests for those men, women and children who would say openly, yes, they were Christians.

Stephen, watching all this from heaven in the special seat reserved for "First Martyr," understood why God had brought him home in such a manner. He had been in the right place at the right time. A spark from Stephen's white-hot zeal, which nothing, not even stones, could put out, had escaped and ignited the heart of the Christian-hating Saul.

It would lie there for a little while until the time was right for it to burst into flame, and when it did, the whole world would be lit up by the fire of Saul's faith. For Saul is known to us now as Paul the Apostle.

Paul

hen the Church was very new, there was a man named Saul who did his best to make the lives of Christians miserable. He was a Jew, a proud and powerful Pharisee, who believed only in the law of Moses. He needed only to hear a whisper of a *possibility* that a Christian was nearby and he would erupt like a just-lit firecracker.

He dug and prodded and sniffed and snorted, like a dog determined to find a buried bone, until he unearthed the doomed believers. Then in an explosion of curses and threats, he sent them on their way to heaven. It is no wonder that Saul the Pharisee became known as the Passionate Persecutor of the People of God.

If Christian mothers had told stories about him to their children, he probably would have sounded as frightful as the giant in *Jack the Giant Killer,* thundering: "Fee, fi, fo, fum, I smell the blood of a Christian-son!" (Or daughter.)

But instead of telling stories, they were busy warning them to beware of a stranger riding a white horse—one who was bald and had fierce blue eyes, a big nose and thick black eyebrows that met together across his forehead. He was also bowlegged, but since he was most often on his horse chasing Christians, hardly anyone noticed.

What he didn't have in looks, Saul made up in spirit and determination. There was no doubt in his mind that whatever he

178

thought, said, or did was absolutely right. He never looked at a problem from two sides and said *maybe,* or *perhaps* he *could* be wrong. He was what you'd call a fanatic, a person who is wildly positive that he is right and positively wild in his way of proving it.

And on top of that, he had a wicked temper. And he was impulsive. And he was touchy as a grouchy porcupine, ready to shoot his quills if anyone disturbed him. His poor parents, they had such a handful! Their hearts must have ached wondering what would ever happen to their headstrong, willful son.

Well, one day about five years after Jesus' death, Saul was ready to shoot off his quills again. He had decided to go up to Damascus to round up those trouble-making Christians and bring back as many as he could find to Jerusalem. So, with a few of his Pharisee friends, Saul galloped off into the sunrise on a journey that would turn his whole world inside out and upside down.

They were clattering along—and then it happened. There was a sudden blinding flash of light, like a lightning bolt that shot across the sky and stayed there. Saul's horse bucked and quivered and whinnied and threw his master to the ground. As he lay there, stunned, a voice came out of the heavens, very deep and very clear: "Saul, *Saul,* do you hear me? Why are you doing this to me?"

Saul was startled but not frightened. He answered this question with another question.

"Who are you, sir?"

And the voice said, "I am Jesus, whom you are persecuting."

Now Saul was frightened. All the terrible things he had done to Christians, all the hatred he had simmering inside against them— what if it had all been wrong? What if it were possible that they *were* the true believers? In that case, he reasoned quickly, it was only fair that God kill him in return. He lay there trembling, waiting for the flash that would end it all.

But there was only this brilliance and the waiting silence. Saul could not stand waiting. He dared to call out in a faint voice, "Lord, what will you have me do?"

The Lord told him to keep on the road to Damascus and, when he arrived there, to go to the house of a man named Judas. Then he said that Saul should join the Christians instead of trying to kill them. He wanted Saul to become a Christian!

Saul almost laughed out loud at such a ridiculous idea. Saul the Persecutor, one of those crazy fools for Christ? But he couldn't even manage a chuckle because he felt strangely excited about it. It seemed so right. He didn't know it then but God had given him his gift of grace. Saul didn't want it, he didn't deserve it, but he *had* it.

Saul thanked God for this second chance and told him he would use all his zeal and energy to work with this grace. He would love and follow Christ as boldly as he had hunted him before. He would be joyful and fearless in telling the world about Christ, no matter where the road and God's will took him.

He pulled himself up and suddenly the brilliance was gone. The voice was gone. The sun had gone too. Everything was black. In a panic, he groped for his horse but could not find him.

"I am blind!" he cried out. Was this to be his punishment for being so cruel? Would he have to work for the Lord without being able to see?

His friends led him to the house of Judas when they got to Damascus. There he stayed for three days, neither eating nor drinking nor seeing. Now there was a Christian named Ananias who also lived in Damascus, and on the night that Saul came to Judas' house, Christ appeared to Ananias in a dream.

He told him to go to Saul and tell him to be baptized. At that, Ananias woke and thought he had had a nightmare. He knew about Saul, the Christian-killer. The Lord couldn't possible want Ananias to visit *him*.

He went back to sleep and the dream came back even stronger. Jesus added, "Go, Ananias, for this man will carry my name before Gentiles and kings and the children of Israel, and I will show him how much he has to suffer for my name."

At the same time Ananias had his dream, Saul had one too.

He saw a man he did not know enter his room and lay his hands upon his eyes and he could see again. He woke and was still lying in his bed thinking about the dream when Ananias came into his room.

Ananias stood by Saul's bed and laid his trembling hands upon Saul's eyes. "Brother Saul," he said, "the Lord Jesus who appeared to you on your journey has sent me so you may have your sight back and be filled with the Holy Spirit!"

Immediately great flakes like scales fell from Saul's eyes and he looked with joy upon Ananias. Yes, he was the man in his dream. Saul embraced him.

Ananias knew Saul now as a brother in Christ. He continued, "The God of our fathers has chosen you to be a witness to all peoples of what you have seen and heard. Why do you tarry? Hurry, arise! Be baptized and washed from your sins, calling on the name of the Lord!"

Saul wasted not a moment. He jumped up, was baptized, and ate a hearty breakfast to celebrate the lifting of darkness from his eyes and his soul.

Then he thought that as long as he was going to have a new life, he would want a new name, and he chose Paul. He immediately went to the synagogue and introduced himself as Paul-who-was-once-Saul and began to preach and praise the Lord he had once hated. Everyone—Jew, Christian, Gentile—was speechless.

Before they had time to make any sense of this, Paul had left Damascus. He went to the desert of Arabia, where he spent the next three years praying and thinking. He wanted to learn about himself and what his special work for the Lord was to be. When he felt he knew, he came back to Damascus, but he was not received with joy.

No one was glad to see him. The disciples were still suspicious of him and didn't trust him. The Pharisees were furious with him for joining the Christians. But Paul paid them no mind and went on preaching with enthusiasm. Gradually the Christians threw away their doubts and accepted him as their brother. He called himself the "13th apostle." (We're so used to thinking of him as Paul the Apostle, it's a small surprise to realize he wasn't one of the original 12.)

Paul was so successful in turning hearts to God that the Pharisees decided the only way to stop him was to kill him. Some disciples overheard the whispered plans and went quickly to tell Paul. His enemies were planning to trap him that very night, so Paul had to work with speed with what he had on hand.

He found a basket in the pantry, a very large wash basket which could have held laundry for a family of 10. He, being small, could just fit into it, so he tucked himself in while the disciples covered him with a red-checked tablecloth.

You might think this basket looked a bit suspicious. You're right. After all, it would have to be a pretty big basket to hold an apostle. But God was with them. Only once did a soldier stop them and ask what was in the basket. The two disciples who were carrying the basket by its handles had a moment of heart flurries.

"Oh, just 42 loaves of Italian bread, 7 strings of salami, and a whole lot of dill pickles for a wedding party," said one disciple, casually. The other whistled and looked up into the air.

The soldier nodded and waved them on. Once they reached the city wall, they hoisted the basket up and lowered it down over the other side by rope. The rope snapped just before Paul landed.

Paul went to Jerusalem and he wasn't welcome there either. So he went back to his hometown of Tarsus and took up his trade of tentmaking. He thought he would wait there until the Lord told him where to go.

Before long Barnabas, a Christian friend, came to him and persuaded him to go with him to Antioch in Syria, where they could preach about Christ to those who didn't know him at all. It was a new challenge, and Paul soaked up challenges like a blotter does ink, so off they went.

They worked for a year in Antioch and, for the first time, Paul had great success. They left a community of Christians behind, the first of many more to come. And Antioch was his jumping-off place. For 20-some more years, he traveled hundreds—thousands—of miles, touching every bustling city, marketplace, or tiny rest-stop watering hole. He convinced an uncountable number of souls to be warmed in God's love and to let it soak in and cover every part of their lives.

He journeyed to Corinth and Ephesus and Thessalonica, and from there to Galatia and Malta and Cyprus. And after he founded churches in all those places, he thought he'd see what he could do in Crete and Athens and Syracuse. Someone once wrote that he planted churches the way Johnny Appleseed planted trees.

When he wasn't on the road, he was writing letters to the brothers and sisters he had left behind in those communities. His letters were those of a loving father, who cared enough about his children to scold them and urge them to do better. He patted them on the back and then tweaked their noses.

He never asked more of them than he did of himself. He was their leader (although sometimes nagging, impatient leader) who could not bear to see anyone poke along the road. He wanted them to stride with great vigor, "pressing on to the goal, to the prize of God's heavenly calling!" There were to be no stops for snoozes or buying popcorn.

Paul's spirit kept his body going. He was sick on and off all his life. He didn't eat what was good for him, and he couldn't bear to waste time sleeping, and his nose was always either nipped by frost or burned by the sun. His nerves never had a moment's rest, for he was always just one jump ahead of the local sheriff who wanted to chase him out of town for disturbing the peace.

Yet, by God's grace, Paul persevered. He tells us that, "Five times I have received at the hands of the Jews forty lashes less one. Three times I have been beaten with rods. Once I was stoned. Three times I have been shipwrecked. A night and a day I have been adrift at sea. In danger of rivers ... robbers ... my own people ..."

Paul loved to tell these stories of his adventures. If sometimes his tales of how he escaped shipwrecks and snakes and jails sound somewhat puffed-up, I don't think he meant to be boastful about himself. Rather, he wanted to show that the glory of his wiggling out of these incredible escapades belongs to God. The only way he could come out on top of them was because Christ was with him and in him.

"It is no longer I who live but Christ who lives in me!" he would explain.

The time came, however, when there would be no last-minute escape. The Emperor Nero decided to silence Paul for good and ordered him beheaded. From his Roman jail Paul wrote his friend Timothy, "I am even now ready to be sacrificed; the time is at hand. But," and you can almost see his eyes light up, "I have fought a good fight; I have finished my course; I have kept the faith!"

And so, on a road outside the gates of Rome, Paul lost his head. I'm sure, if he had had the pen and paper and time, he would have recorded that it was of much more importance that he lost his heart to Christ on that road to Damascus many years ago.

If you'd like to curl up some rainy afternoon and read Paul's letters for yourself, you will find them at the end of the New Testament in the Bible. Don't worry if you don't understand them all or trip over the names of cities. You will find some small part which you feel Paul was writing for *you,* as well as those long-ago Christians.

He will remind you that "whatever you do, work at it with your whole being and do it for the Lord!"

For the Lord and not for the reward, which is nice but not necessary. So when you shovel snow, scour the bathtub because the bather before you didn't, study French, empty the kitty litter, make Jello, mind your whiny sister or write a thank-you to Aunt Kathy who always sends you underwear for your birthday—don't expect money or praise or a favor in return. Do it with your whole being for the Lord.

Like Paul, *press on* to the heavenly goal!

More Saints Budding Everywhere

Spring/Summer

STA 9n 3
April 2007

A Litany for the Garden

When ladybugs bloom
On the kitchen sill,
And bears come out
In the April chill,

The time has come
We know in our marrow
To go and fetch
The rusty wheelbarrow

And pile it high
With garden needs:
With tools and twine
And stakes and seeds,
And leaves and lime
To quell the weeds.

But even before
We rake the stones
We call on the saints
To shake their bones.

They come on the run,
This heavenly crew,
To bless the earth
With holy dew.

O saintly ones
With thumbs of green!
Look with love
On the lima bean.

Protect the pea
And the Chantenay carrot
From slugs and rot
And the mealy-mouthed maggot!

Isidore, I implore
Your kind guarantee
To hold off the hoar,
Bring on the bee,

Coax the wind
And sun and heat
To swell the grains
Of oat and wheat.

Fiacre, please guide
My uncertain hoe
From zigzag ditch
To respectable row.

St. Barnaby, kindly
Blow the whistle
On advancing columns
Of unruly thistle.

And Blase, please tame
Its cousin teasel.
Likewise, dear Martin,
The nightstalking weasel.

Golden girl Clare
Will shower the sun,
And when we need rain,
Odo's the one.

Laughing Bridget's
The saint with the power
To fling free the carpet
Of dandelion flower.

If you would plant flax,
Unsure as to how,
Call upon Stanislaus,
Who lived in Cracow.

There's Lawrence for grapes,
And Botulf for turnips,
Margaret for poppies—
But who, Lord, for parsnips?

St. Philbert, of course,
Is for nuts of all sorts.

There is no end
Of this loving bunch
Who till the plot
For our free lunch.

You'd think the garden
Was a soul
Which they must guard
From moth and mole,

And mice who chew.
If the soil be sour,
No matter. They just smile
And pray and work by the hour,

Weeding and mulching
And warming by hand
This unlikely spot
Of promised land.

Note: Most of the saints mentioned in this "Litany of the Garden" are celebrated in the course of spring and summer: Stanislaus (April 11), Isidore the Farmer (May 15), Bridget (July 23), Lawrence (August 10) and Clare (August 11). And Botulf (June 17), Odo of Canterbury (July 3), Philbert (actually, Phil*i*bert, August 20), Fiacre (September 1) and Margaret of Hungary (June 10), while not included in the current Roman Calendar, have been traditionally celebrated in this season. Blase (February 3) and Martin de Porres (November 3) are the exceptions.

Catherine of Siena

April 29

here was once a young woman who spoke with such wisdom everyone stopped to listen. Kings and soldiers and princes and popes waited for her every word. And she not only spoke, she sent letters by the buckets, hundreds and hundreds filled with strong advice sweetly offered. They were so powerful whoever read them would slap the table, jump up and say, "Yes, yes, she's right, and by God's grace, I shall do it!"

Her name was Catherine of Siena. She was the 24th child and youngest daughter of Jacopo and Lapa Benincasa, who were wooldyers in the town of Siena in Italy. Can you imagine being the youngest child in a family of that size? Catherine liked to be alone and learned very early to find her own amusement. What she liked to do best was to close the door to the tiny room at the top of the stairs and sit on the red brick floor, as if it were an enchanted island, and dream and pray.

The next best thing was to climb up and down the stairs leading to her room, kneeling on each stair as she said a Hail Mary. Her mother didn't mind at all. At least it kept her out of mischief. "But be careful coming down, little one. I have enough problems without your banging your head!"

Sometimes her older brother Stephen took her out to play hopscotch or count dandelions or visit the store where they sold lemon ices. One evening just before supper, they were outside watching the sunset over the Church of St. Dominic on top of the hill. The sky was splashed with gold and scarlet and pink. As Catherine soaked in the beauty to save in her memory, she saw more than brilliant colors.

Catherine saw our Lord on his throne, surrounded by his disciples Peter, Paul and John, all shining and joyous in splendid robes. Jesus stretched out his hand and blessed the little girl. Catherine stood motionless, as if she had turned to stone. Stephen shook her roughly. He was very frightened. Catherine was not breathing, yet she *couldn't* be dead standing up. Oh, what would their mother say! He shook her again, urgently.

She gave a start and quickly looked back at the sky. The vision was gone. She began to cry and sob and beat on Stephen angrily. "Why did you do that? Now he's gone. Oh, if you had seen what I saw, you wouldn't have shaken me!"

Poor Stephen! He had seen nothing and thought Catherine had been out in the sun too long.

But Catherine knew what she had seen was real. Jesus had come to her and invited her to be his. From that moment, she vowed to belong to Christ alone. Everything she did would be at his bidding. This was a secret between Catherine and our Lord for the next six years. No one suspected. She was such a laughing child, running here and there like a golden bird; no one believed she ever had a serious thought in her sunny blond head. Everyone called her Joy, because that is what she was.

When she was 12, her mother brushed out her golden hair and said soon they would be looking for the right husband for their little girl. Catherine jumped up and said, "No, Mother, I will marry no one. I have already promised myself to Jesus."

Now Jacopo and Lapa were very good people. They were generous and loving in the care of their 24 blessings from God, but they would not hear of such nonsense from a child! What did she know of life or God or *anything*? They asked a priest to come and talk with her. By the time he was through, he was convinced she was right. He whispered to her as he left, "If you are serious, cut off your hair."

Now a young woman's hair in those days was truly her crowning glory. The longer her hair, the more beautiful she was considered. If, by some mishap, it was cut off, no one would want to marry her. So Catherine grabbed her scissors and chopped and chopped until she looked ghastly.

Her parents were furious. How dare she ruin their plans! To bring her to her senses, they dismissed all the servants and turned the work of the house over to Catherine. So she cooked and swept and washed and hung out laundry for 26 people. She did it without sulking or talking back. After all, she thought, the martyrs had worse things to bear than peeling potatoes for a large family.

They took away her tiny room so she would have no more time for her silly dreaming. When she sniffled a little about this to our Lord, he told her that she must turn in to the cell of her heart, where she would always find him. He reminded her that he was always with her, strengthening her. She didn't need her room for their visits.

One day, when she was scraping the burnt crust off the roast pan with her finger nail, her father walked in and saw a white dove nestled on her shoulder, his soft wing brushing her hair. By God's grace, his mind was opened and he knew the dove was the Holy Spirit. He put his arms around his little girl and promised she would never have to marry anyone on this earth.

"Let her serve her Bridegroom in complete freedom," he told his wife. "We could never obtain so honorable a marriage for her. Instead of a mortal man, we have been given the immortal God-made-man!"

For the next three years, Catherine lived in her little room, going out only for Mass at the convent church. She prayed, mostly, and visited with our Lord. Then God gave her the gift of reading. She didn't learn to read as we do, starting with the alphabet. She just sat down one day, opened a page of the Psalms and rattled it off as if she had written it herself. Now she could read her prayers as well as think them.

One night Jesus came and told her it was a very special visit. He put a gold ring on her finger, which meant she was truly his forever.

She promised him, with tears in her eyes, "As the fish arise in the sea, so thou art in me and I am in Thee."

And now, our Lord said, it was time for Catherine to go out and serve him in the sick and poor so they might come to him. Catherine said she'd rather not. She was afraid of the world; she had been away from it so long. And if she were too busy with the world outside, she would be separated from him.

"Catherine," said our Lord, "you know that I have given you two commandments, to love me and to love your neighbor. I ask that you walk not on one but two feet and fly to heaven on two wings."

So right then and there, she told him that her trust in him was stronger than her fear of what awaited her in the world. She combed her hair (which had grown back), straightened her apron and went down to dinner. Everyone was so surprised they could hardly eat. They all talked at once and Catherine asked would someone please pass the lima beans, and it was just like old times, her mother sighed wistfully.

Catherine was 18 now, old enough to become a member of the Dominican Third Order. Even though she was a nun, she still lived at home instead of in a community.

Catherine took her job working with the sick in earnest. She worked at the leper hospital with such love and tenderness that no one ever knew that she couldn't stand sickness and dirt and the unpleasant smells that went with both. She had a passion for clean rooms with clean white curtains and fresh air blowing in the windows, and yet she worked in windowless wards filled with unbathed bodies and soiled sheets as if she were strolling through a bower of honeysuckle.

She took care of the most abandoned and unpleasant patients. At first they resented her because she was pretty, healthy, young—all the things they were not. They blamed God for all their woes and sometimes cursed him. But Catherine ignored this. She looked for the good in everyone and she usually found it. Under the bad temper, greed and just plain meanness, she saw our Lord. And as she washed and soothed and fed grumpy old ladies, she would ask him to

heal and touch their hearts as well as their bodies.

There was an old woman named Cecca who was as mean as she was sick. Meaner! Nobody went near her. Nothing could please her. The soup was too hot, the eggs were too hard, the water too soapy, her braids too tight, and would somebody *please* cut her toenails?

She made fun of Catherine to the others and called her an old maid. "There's nothing else for her to do but take care of us since she couldn't catch a husband. She ought to be glad we give her something to do!"

Catherine let the meanness roll off her heart like butter off a hot griddle. But sometimes, when she wished they would be just a little nicer, our Lord would say to her, "Catherine, I have two crowns, one of gold and one of thorns. Which would you rather have in this life? I will save the other for eternity."

She chose the crown of thorns. After all, if our Lord could die for his enemies, she could bear with Cecca!

One morning Catherine went to the hospital and, as she always did, bathed Cecca's bleeding fingers and bandaged them. Cecca began to screw up her face into a black look. But then her eyes widened. She covered her face with her stumps of hands and began weeping—for when she had looked at Catherine, she had seen instead the face of the Lord.

"Forgive me," she begged the young woman. "I am a cranky old woman who has forgotten how to say thank you. Never again shall I forget!" And she didn't.

Besides nursing the sick, Catherine buried the dead, visited prisoners and became Siena's best peacemaker. Her ability to patch up fights and find the best solutions became so well-known that people talked of her in Florence and Naples and Rome. Her secret was in her complete trust in God to advise and counsel her. She would listen most carefully to both sides of a story and then listen to what God said to her. Then she would tell straight out, without fear, what must be done to set a life or a country in order.

Very often, she sent letters (over 400 of them). Since she had never learned to write, she dictated them to her secretaries. She had three young noblemen who were part of a band of people who followed her everywhere. These poets, artists and scholars were called the *Caterinati*. They rarely left her side and were like daily newspapers, reporting her latest sayings and good deeds. They called her Mama and, indeed, she treated them like her children.

She treated everyone like a loving Italian mama, one who is used to being obeyed. She coaxed and scolded and teased and embraced and, of course, gave orders. But she did it so charmingly, especially in her letters, few could resist her suggestions. She wrote to kings and princes and priests and popes with advice on how to bring about peace in their country and in the Church.

At that time, there were always disagreements popping up over something, and God's Word could barely be heard above the clamor of war cries and the clattering hooves of charging horses. But before there could be any peace, Catherine knew, the pope (who was then living in Avignon in France) must come home to Rome, where the head of the Church should be.

She wrote to Pope Gregory with the sweetness of a mother and the force of an archangel. She called him her "sweet babbo" and sent him candied orange peel in a tea tin for a Christmas present with a note that read, "Beyond the first bitter taste you will find sweetness, as one finds sweetness in the will of the Lord." Then she added that it was the Lord's will that he return to Rome. And he did.

When that pope died, she wrote the new one, Pope Urban, and asked if she might come to Rome to live. He said, "Yes, my daughter, we need you!" He told the cardinals and princes and other important people to listen to the "little woman," *picco donzella,* who had the spiritual wisdom to save the Church.

Catherine went on preaching and teaching with her letters, and when she was 33, she died. In her short life, she had grown from a timid girl who did not want to leave her little room to a fearless advisor to the popes and a Doctor of the Church, as honored as Thomas Aquinas. On the evening that she died, she looked at the sky and caught her breath. It was a wild sky of molten gold and scarlet and rose streaked with purple. It was a sky the like of which she had not seen since she was six years old.

And there in the center of the glorious color was the vision of her youth—Jesus with John and Paul and Peter around him and Mary smiling over them all!

Our Lord reached out his hand, and Catherine hurried to grasp it. She would not lose the vision this time, for now she was part of it.

Saints at Harvest-Time

Autumn

With September begins the golden time of autumn, the prime time of the year for nature and the Church. The gardens and trees and fields have flowered and fruited, and the Seed once buried in a garden near Calvary has risen and thrust out vines that cover the world.

The seasons of the year and the liturgy of the Church co-exist and merge. Both have birth in the fickle days of spring. In nature's realm the seed catalogs of winter plant the dream in our hearts. Inspired, we go forth with seeds of unknown quality to sow the dream in half-frozen ground. We plan and wait, then plant and pray. We have our troubles: The soil is acid, the deer are hungry, the sun parches. But the stubborn seedlings persist, and we coax and guard and pray again.

Finally, it is autumn, and we are so proud! By the Feast of Christ the King, all is glory. The fruit of the vine is ready and our cup runneth over. The harvest is in!

So, too, is the harvest of our King. The first, most perfect Seed was dropped into the thorny, bloody soil of Good Friday. Nothing could stop the shoot from cracking the hardened, fallow soil. The saints were its seed pods blown by the wind of Providence.

They were healers, scholars, queens and poets, mystics, psychics, businessmen and barbers. Some were animal-tamers. But all were gardeners of the spirit.

They put first things first. They trusted absolutely. They loved completely. And their impossible garden burst with abundance and succulent sweetness. With infinite delight, they (and we) gather the harvest to cram the cupboards and pantries and barns of the King.

We know that someday we too shall bequeath our harvest to Christ our King. May he, in his graciousness, declare it delectable.

Cosmas and Damian

September 26

nce upon a time, there were twin brothers who did everything together from the moment they were born. They took their first steps, running to their mother, at the same time. They woke at 6 a.m. together, rubbed their eyes and scratched their heads together, and always wanted Cream of Wheat for breakfast on the same days. They even made holes in the toes of their socks at the same time. So when one brother said, "I think I'm going to be a saint," the other, of course, replied, "Why, I was just thinking the same thing!"

Their names were Cosmas and Damian and they were born into a wealthy fmily of Arabia nearly 300 years after Christ died. When they were toddlers, bouncing about like two peas in a pod, their father died. They missed him terribly. Even though they were Christians and tried to be brave, the boys would go to their rooms and cry in the dark because they didn't have a father.

Their mother told them to dry their eyes because they *did* have a father who was the King of Heaven. Since he was a king, they were royal children and must always act as a king's sons. They must fill their lives with noble deeds and help the weak and the sick and the lonely.

The boys grew up, enjoying their secret and trying to live up to it. They were sons of a king! They decided to become doctors—together, of course—doctors for the poor as well as the rich. Not only were there uncountable poor people in their land, but also a great deal of sickness of all variety. And there were not enough doctors. Only the very wealthy could afford to have a doctor living in their palaces, and they certainly didn't want poor people coming there, scuffing up the floors and putting dirty fingermarks on the walls.

So Cosmas and Damian studied for years with the most learned men of medicine. They were taught how to set broken limbs and lower fevers and massage away aches. They discovered the herbs and grasses and flowers that would help heal and cure, and they learned how sick and unhappy minds often made the body act the same way.

They cared for rich and poor alike, and even for animals. After all, as Damian said, "People can speak and complain of their sickness. But those dumb creatures, also made by our King, can only suffer in silence."

The brothers taught people not to fuss over themselves or take to their beds at the first sign of sniffles but to be sensible and use God's natural gifts. They carried wild horseradish roots and cloves of garlic for people with clogged-up heads. "There you are," they'd tell them as they wheezed and sneezed, "*this* will clean out your sinuses!"

So their days were busy from sunrise to sunset. They mixed yarrow with cobwebs to stop bleeding wounds, and put castor oil on warts and corns and bathed sore eyes with eyebright tea. Wherever they were, people found them and came in a steady stream: ladies with headaches and carpenters with smashed thumbs, girls with hiccups and boys with black eyes, a bear with a bee-stung nose, a camel with a cramp. No one, person or beast, was ever turned away.

The brothers asked only one thing of their patients: They could make no payment for their healing. Cosmas and Damian told them it was the work which God had given them to do, and as God asked no payment for the gifts he gave, neither would they.

Sometimes it is harder to receive a gift than to give one, especially when you are so grateful you want to do *something* to say thank you. One day a woman whom the brothers had cured of a dizziness, which made her tilt to one side and feel as though the sky was falling in on her, could not contain her happiness.

She offered them a sack with three fresh eggs in it, begging them to please accept it.

Cosmas walked away, and the woman turned to Damian. "Please, sir, you have cured my dizzy tilt and I can see the world as it is again. Won't you please take these eggs and enjoy them? I ask you in Jesus' name!"

When Damian heard that, his heart was touched. How could he refuse her without being rude to our Lord? So he took the eggs and brought them home. When Cosmas saw them, he became very angry. For the first time in their lives, the brothers did not agree.

"Damian," Cosmas asked, "how could you do this? You know we made a vow never to take payment for any good we do. How could you take these eggs from that poor woman?"

He turned from his brother, refusing to share the room with him, and went outdoors to sleep.

That night, God crept into Cosmas' dreams, into his very heart, and asked, "Cosmas, my son, why are you so angry at your brother?"

"Lord," he answered, "You know why. He went back on his word. You know our vow!"

"Cosmas, you are thinking just with your head. Do not be so stiff-necked and proud that you must follow the letter of your own law. Was it not in my name that Damian took the eggs? The woman gave them in love for me and in thanks to you for letting me work through you. Don't you see? Your brother is wiser than you."

Cosmas woke and thought with his heart. He went quickly to his brother and gave him a bear hug, which woke Damian up very quickly. Damian forgave him, for he understood.

(Sometimes we decide to do something for Christ and won't budge an inch because that's the way *we* want it, even if we make other people unhappy. We may decide to offer up chocolate chip cookies because we *love* chocolate chip cookies. And then we visit a lonely old lady who loves to bake cookies for company. Her eyes light up with pleasure when she offers us one and we must decide quickly. Do we say, "No, thank you," so we can say with pride, "I never slipped *once*"? Or do we think of her feelings and eat the cookies, telling her how absolutely delicious they are? We must decide, as Damian did, to act as our Lord would in the same situation.)

The brothers' fame began to spread throughout Arabia, and this angered the ruler, who was not a Christian. These brothers would turn the whole country Christian if they went about healing and comforting and doing good. They must be stopped, he decided.

He ordered Cosmas and Damian to be seized and cast into the sea. They were hustled off to a cliff overlooking the cold gray water. Here the soldiers bound their hands and feet and threw them into the wild, churning waves.

Immediately, so they say, the sea turned quiet and blue and the wind became gentle as a sigh. The brothers rose to the surface of the water, their hands and feet freed, and walked toward the shore, each led by an angel who surrounded them with a protecting light.

The ruler was very angry at this, and a bit frightened. He certainly didn't want the Christians to prove that there was a God who cared enough about them to send his angels to guard them. He ordered that they be cast into a roaring fire and thought that would be the last of them.

As soon as Cosmas and Damian were thrown into the flaming mass, the fire flickered and grew dim, until only a faint gray ash was left. The brothers stepped out — not burnt to a crisp, but just nicely pink and healthy-looking.

Then the ruler, very, very angry by now, ordered them to be bound to crosses and stoned to death by the soldiers. But as the stones flew through the air, they turned back and bounced off the soldiers who had thrown them. Before long, the ground was littered with men groaning and holding their heads. Cosmas whispered to Damian, "Somebody should send for a doctor!"

Once again, the ruler tried. He ordered archers to shoot their arrows into the hearts of the brothers, but the arrows also changed direction and returned to chase the archers. They dropped their bows and fell to the ground, hoping the arrows would zoom by and miss them.

Finally, the ruler declared that these men were magicians. Since magic was made by the mind, he would simply relieve them of their minds. He ordered Cosmas and Damian to be beheaded, and so they were.

Cosmas and Damian lost their heads for God. They had given him their hearts long ago; and now, bodies and souls, they came back altogether to him. And they didn't stop their healing just because they were in heaven. They were incurable curers. People who prayed to them were healed, or the brothers would appear to the sick in their dreams and tell them where to find valerian root for their nerves and wild ginger for their upset stomachs.

Cosmas and Damian have left us more than the stories of their healing. They have taught us how to act as children of the King. They have shown us that we are to think first of serving God and his people, to use our talents and not be concerned what we get in the way of money or honor.

When we do something we know is absolutely wonderful, we don't stand around with our hands in our pockets, waiting to be told how absolutely wonderful we are. Royal children don't need rewards. We've already inherited heaven!

Vincent de Paul

September 27

nce upon a time, there was a boy named Vincent who tried to fool God. He thought he could pretend to be someone he wasn't, and no would ever know. Because he was a poor boy who hated being poor, he told himself that he would become a priest. Then he would have a comfortable life, with plenty of food and his own home, and everyone would look up to him. He would be the master instead of the servant.

But Vincent forgot that God has a sense of humor that can turn the tables on the best of plans. He listened to the thoughts in Vincent's mind and chuckled. "Very well, my son, you shall be a priest. More than that, you will be a saint, my saint of the poor!"

Vincent, who had been born in a peasant family in France, wanted so much to escape his life of poverty that he lay awake nights on his straw cot, planning ways to change it. He did not like tending sheep and pigs all day at the mercy of the wind and sun and rain. He wanted to be comfortable, to wear clean, warm clothes and eat roast chicken and drink good red wine — just like the village priest!

There was no reason he couldn't be a priest. He was smart and he wasn't wicked even if he wasn't very holy either. And in return for this good life, he would do everything he was supposed to do: He would say Mass and baptize babies and bless the vineyards and visit the old ladies of the parish, who would give him French bread and sausage to take home. It would be a good life for everybody.

So Vincent worked hard and before he knew it, he was 24 years old and had been ordained a priest. His dream had come true. Then one fine spring day, he went on a business trip to Marseilles, a seaport town. He finished his work early and decided to come home by boat, since he had the time to enjoy it. The wind was calm and the sun bright. What a pleasant afternoon he would have!

But within the hour, his happiness turned to fear. His heart nearly stopped in fright. The boat was seized and captured by Turkish pirates, who took over the wheel and steered it in the opposite direction to Tunisia, where the passengers would be sold as slaves.

God had begun to play his joke in a rather rough fashion. Vincent, who had been heading for a life of comfort, was led by a chain about his neck to the center of town where merchants could buy the captive they wanted. He was bought first by a fisherman, who then sold him to a doctor, who sold him to a farmer. He and the farmer became friends (Vincent discovered he had once been a Christian), and they decided to try to slip out of the country together. They waited and planned for 10 months before they had the chance to steal a boat and escape in the night to France.

In the two years he had been a slave, God's grace had sparked the beginning of a change in Vincent's heart. The hardships, the struggles, the sufferings of the slaves had stirred something in his soul. He understood them. He had been poor; how could he ever turn his back on that life and not try to change it? He had been able to help the suffering poor in a foreign land. Should he not do the same for his own peasant countrymen in France?

So he came to Paris when he was 27 and met a holy priest named Father Pierre de Berulle, who would guide him to his life's work. Father Pierre saw something special in this young man and felt that God had a definite mission for him, even if he didn't know what it was. When he heard that a wealthy family was in need of a priest for their household, he was sure this was a job for Vincent. So off went the young priest to the household of the de Gondi family.

The de Gondis owned magnificent homes in town and in the country, with huge estates of woods and gardens and trout streams. Vincent was their chaplain and the tutor for the children and he helped in the physical and spiritual care of the servants and workers who took care of the family.

There were so many workers, Vincent banded them together into one big parish. Madame de Gondi approved of this. It relieved her conscience to know that the peasants for whom the family was responsible were being cared for. Soon the work became almost too much for one man. Vincent realized this was work for a special group of priests, a different kind of order (or "company" as he called them), who would devote themselves to the care of poor country people. They should live in a community but not be separated from the world.

He spoke of this to Madame de Gondi, who immediately gathered up a bundle of money and told him to go ahead and *do it*. So he did. He organized a band of priests who would live and work among the poor and called them the Congregation of the Missions (or Vincentians, as we know them now). He, and they, then helped the people of the parish remember that they were brothers and sisters with one Father. They sought out the needy and helped them. Everyone. "Remember," Vincent told them, "that our Lord said, 'Whatsoever you do to these, the least of my brethren, you do to me.' "

The new company found an old estate in Paris which was called St. Lazare because it had once been used to take care of lepers. For 28 years, this was Vincent's headquarters and home. Here he directed his "sons" (and later his "daughters," the Sisters of Charity), wrote his letters, held retreats, and thought up plans to make a better life for the poor.

Before the Sisters of Charity came the Ladies of Charity. These were a group of wealthy, aristocratic women of Paris who were brought together by Vincent's friend Louise de Marillac. Louise had been shaken by the fire of this zealous young priest, who called for the rich to consider their cold and hungry brothers and sisters. She and the ladies were gracious and gave parties and teas to raise money for the poor, and that helped.

But the Ladies were not nurses and had families of their own to tend to. So Louise gathered together and taught young women from the country, who became nurses and teachers and household workers. They were the first band of sisters dedicated to taking care of God's poor. The Sisters of Charity, like the Vincentians, were to live in a community but work in the city with the sick and needy. Vincent wanted no collection of nuns who shut themselves away from the world.

"Your convent will be the house of the sick," he said; "your cell, a hired room; your cloister, the streets of the city or the wards of the hospital."

Soon the Sisters were working everywhere, in hospitals, orphanages, prisons, even in armies. Vincent's "companies" soon became known outside France and spread throughout Europe, Africa and, eventually, America. Then, 200 years after Vincent died, Frederic Ozanam formed the Society of St. Vincent de Paul, a gathering of Catholic laity which continues the practice of loving charity as given to them by "Monsieur Vincent," as he came to be called by the people of Paris.

They loved him as much as he loved them and the city itself. He came to know Paris first as a young priest on horseback, discovering every abandoned child, every beggar or convict who needed help. Then, when he could no longer ride, he walked and poked about with a cane. He loved every inch of his city. He became the priest of a small church to which fishermen, farmers and laborers came. The little church is still standing, and in its garden is a very old tree said to have been planted by Monsieur Vincent himself.

He sometimes tried the patience of those who worked with him, for he was not a naturally good-humored man. He was impatient and quick-tempered and, "but for divine grace," he admitted, "I would have been in temper hard and repellent, rough and crabbed." He was short and squat, with a broad jaw and short beard. His dark brown eyes shone from under black brows that were heavy as an awning. And his nose was very large and like a bulb.

Sometimes he was slow in making a decision. He always

wanted to be sure that what he wanted to do was the will of God. He would not be pushed. "Do not tread on the heels of Providence, who is our guide," he would say. But once he made up his mind that something was God's will, he couldn't be stopped from putting his thoughts into action.

Vincent's idea of charity was that people should take care of each other, person to person, as they saw the need. He didn't believe in leaving it to a government or charity far away. He did believe that the parish and the priest should be the center of our lives, not just on Sunday but every moment; that way we would remember that we are all members of a single family and children of the same heavenly Father.

He gave whatever he had to anyone, without worrying whether it was going to the "right" people. They were all the "right" people. Slaves, orphans, the rejected and despised—all were in his care. "In a poor man," he said, "I do not notice his rough outside, his coarseness . . . , but I look at the reverse . . . . I see nothing save the Son of God, poor by his own choice."

Vincent showed us *how* to give. It is not enough to give money for a poor baby in Bolivia. Good, but not *enough*. We must also think of our neighbor who may have nothing left on his shelves but half a box of soggy cornflakes and a can of spinach and is too proud to let anyone know his stomach is hurting. As you sit here, munching a cracker with peanut butter, it is hard to imagine anyone being that hungry. But *try*. Try to imagine for Sunday dinner a can of spinach that looks like wet, dead seaweed. And that is it. And for Monday's dinner, limp cornflakes.

Vincent sought out the old and lonely (and the young and lonely) and gave them eggs and milk and cabbage and cheese to go with the spinach. He gave himself, his company, his caring. If someone needed a coat, he took off his and gave it. (And he didn't stop to cut off the buttons or the lining in case he might use them sometime.) And when rich people gave him old shoes, he would ask them to make sure they came in pairs. "You know," he would smile, "you'd be surprised to see how few people there are with one foot!" He asked them to give with their whole hearts, and not just to give things they wouldn't use themselves, for what was the sacrifice in that?

Vincent was very much an ordinary man. He saw no visions, performed no miracles, changed nothing but himself. The boy who vowed he would never be poor became the man who chose his home in the midst of the poor.

By the time he reached heaven, he had lost all desire to become the comfortable master of the manor. He had found his place instead as God's handyman, the holy caretaker who patched up frostbitten lives.

Monsieur Vincent, keep us from ever being too comfortable, and give us the grace to be caretakers, too!

The Heavenly Helpers

September 29

hey say our Lord
On his throne in heaven
Is circled by angels
In a ring of seven.

Of this holy band
Three we know well:
Michael and Gabriel
And, of course, Raphael.

What did they do,
These angelic three,
Who touched the earth
Infrequently?

Michael the Avenger banished Satan,
Who preened himself as Prince,
Flung him from heaven to the pit of hell,
And he's been there ever since.
Michael the Protector
Saved Isaac from the knife,
Scattered death on Egypt

To give the Jews life.
Michael the Guardian
Warned Joseph to flee in the dark
To foil cruel Herod
Before the song of the lark.

Gabriel brought tidings
Of the first Christmas morn,
With a vision to Zachary
Of John-to-be-born.
He called on Mary,
As she knelt in the sod,
And gently addressed her
As *Mother of God!*
And when Jesus was born
Gabriel's trumpet shattered the night
And he cheered the shepherds
Cowed in fright.
"Rejoice, fear not,"
His song sang out bold,
"Your Savior is here—
Come out of the cold!"

And Raphael the Healer
To blind Tobias gave sight,
Then walked as guardian
With his son, day and night.
Raphael saved the son
From a monstrous fish,
Then led him to Sarah,
The bride he had wished.
And when Our Lord wept
In Gethsemani's wood,
Raphael consoled him

And blotted the blood.

So if you tangle with Satan
And must do battle,
Call on Michael
So your teeth won't rattle.

And if you bring tidings
By song or by quote,
Gabriel will clear out
The frogs in your throat.

And if you must go
On a trip of import,
Go with Raphael,
Heavenly escort.

Don't forget
These angelic three!
They wait for your call
Or sob or plea,
As they sit on their pins
In eternity.

Therese

October 1

nce upon a time, there was a little girl who was determined to have her own way. When she wanted something, she wanted all of it, no bits or pieces or sips or samples. She wanted *the whole thing,* whether it was a cookie or a box of ribbons or her parents' attention. And because she was the baby of the family, she usually got it.

So when Therese (that was her name) decided that the one thing she wanted in this life was to be a saint, nothing could stop her. She didn't say, "Well, maybe tomorrow, or the day after when I start to feel holy, I'll start," or "When I enter the convent and have time to pray a lot, I'll think about it." She used everything, the whole of her life, for holiness from that moment on.

Therese was like every baby sister you've ever known. She was fussed over and coddled and shown off, with good reason. She was quite pretty, with a mass of golden curls and blue-gray eyes. She had such a way of commanding attention, her father called her his Little Queen. But she was such a charming child people smiled even as they did exactly as she wished.

Her full name was Marie Frances Therese and she was the youngest child of Louis and Zelie Martin. Her father was a well-to-do clockmaker and her mother made the beautiful lace for which their town of Alencon was noted. Her parents loved each other deeply, almost as much as they loved God. When they married, their first prayer was for many children who would become saints.

They gathered a nice large houseful, nine in all. Four children died when they were babies, but their parents did not grieve. They were graced with a faith that helped them rejoice that their little ones had already gained heaven and would be waiting to greet them when they arrived. And, after all, they did have five daughters here on earth to raise.

The eldest was Marie, followed by Pauline, and then Leonie and Celine and, finally, Therese. The baby of the family never wanted for someone to push her on the swing, tie her shoelaces or get her a drink during the night. Sometimes it seemed as if she had five mothers taking care of her.

The sister she loved most dearly was Celine. They did everything together. They giggled and had secrets and made hand shadows on the walls and teased each other. Often Therese would climb out of her bed at night and jump in with Celine. In the morning she would hug her tightly and beg the maid, Louise, to let her stay with her big sister. "Can't you see we are like two little white chickens and we must always be together?"

Once, when Therese was small, Leonie brought a basket of outgrown toys and said she and Celine might choose one apiece, since they had been good that morning. Celine took forever to pick, and just when Therese was about to burst with impatience, she chose a fuzzy white rabbit. Therese quickly snatched the basket out of her hands and held it tightly to her chest. "I choose *everything!*" she snapped, and marched out of the room with her prize.

Of course she brought it back in a matter of moments, for even though she was sometimes selfish, she was just as quick to be sorry and smother someone she had hurt with kisses.

The Martins were a happy family, full of love and delight in having each other around. But when Therese was four, her mother died and their lives were changed forever. Pauline became her Little Mother (and Marie was Celine's). Their father grieved for his wife, even though he knew that she was happy in heaven. He did not want to stay in their home, so full of family memories, so he sold his business and moved his family to the town of Lisieux.

He found a lovely old house called *Les Buissonets* (The Elms) which perked up everyone's spirits. It was a perfect home for romping and growing up in, with secret nooks and window seats to curl up on and read or dream or pray. Marie ran the house and Pauline took charge of teaching the others their lessons and prayers. She would read aloud to them at night, stories from the Gospels or the lives of the saints, and Therese's soul soaked it up as a thirsty rose would water.

When Therese was nine, Pauline left The Elms to enter the convent of the Carmelites at Lisieux. Therese thought her heart would break to lose her Little Mother. Then, with her whole-hearted determination, she decided that this would be her life and that she would enter the convent also. She had known in her heart for some time that God wanted her to give her life completely to him. She wanted with all her being to offer her life for poor souls who were hurt or lonely or angry or full of hate, and who had no one to pray for them. But she had a while to wait.

When she was 14, her sister Marie joined Pauline in the convent, and soon after Leonie left to become a Visitation nun. That left only Celine and Therese home to take care of their father. The desire to become a Carmelite had grown stronger until Therese could not bear to keep it to herself any longer. She had to go as soon as possible!

But what of her father? How could she leave him while he was still so sad from her mother's death? Gently, almost fearfully, she told him how she felt. Her father drew her to him, and with tears in his eyes (and his heart no doubt aching), Louis Martin told his daughter of the great joy she had given him with her news. It could not have been easy for him to lose his Little Queen, but he remembered that he and Zelie had prayed for children who would someday be saints. How could he hold this eager one back?

But even though he was willing and gave Therese his blessing, the nuns at the convent, her parish priest and the Bishop were not so agreeable. They said she could not enter the convent until she was *at least* 18 years old. Since their word was final, the only one who could change their minds was the Pope himself.

Very well, then, they would make the pilgrimage to Rome. Therese and Celine and their father arrived in Rome with the request for an audience. It was granted and Therese, who was not yet 15, became frightened at what she was about to do. She was awed at the thought of speaking with the Pope and knew she would stammer and stutter and never get the words out right. But without his help she felt she would never get to join her sisters in the convent.

As she inched closer and closer in the line to see the Pope, she caught the eye of the priest from her parish who had refused her permission to enter the Carmelites. He must have read her mind, for he immediately announced in a loud voice that no one was to speak to the Holy Father.

Her heart beat loudly. She could hear it in her ears and feel it in her throat. She knew this was meant for her. She looked back at Celine. "Go ahead and speak!" urged her sister. Therese's turn had come and she went to her knees in front of the Pope.

"Most Holy Father," she pleaded, as fast as she could, "I want to ask you a great favor."

He bent down, his head almost touching hers, and his dark eyes met her wet ones.

"Please let me enter Carmel now even though I am only 15!" The priest behind the Pope was startled and angry. He interrupted Therese. "Your Holiness, this girl wishes to enter Carmel and her superiors are already going over the question."

"Very well, my child," said the Pope, "you must do what the superiors decide."

This wasn't enough for Therese. She wanted more, a definite *yes.* "*Please,* Holy Father! If you said yes, everyone else would be willing."

He gazed at her and said, feeling her hands clutching his knees, "Well, well, you will enter if it is God's will."

Her time was up, but Therese did not move. She prayed for the right words to move the Holy Father's heart. Two guards came over to lead her away, but she still would not move. She looked as stubborn as a dog who will not give up a bone. She clung tightly to the Pope's knees while the guards tried to tug her away. Finally the priest joined them, and the three men finally pulled her off and carried her out of the church.

Therese was hurt and puzzled. Surely Jesus had told her that he wanted her at Carmel. Thus, she reasoned simply, she must get there by any means. But she was beginning slowly to realize that she must let go of her strong will. She must let go and let God take care of it; she must trust him completely as a little child would her father.

She decided that she would offer herself to the Child Jesus as a plaything, a little ball to do with exactly as he liked. He could pick up this ball, throw it down, or let it roll far from him, but in the end, he would hold it close to his heart and never let it go again. Right now, she felt like a very sad little ball that had lost its bounce and was full of holes and abandoned.

But Jesus came quickly to rescue his plaything. The Bishop did give his permission, and when she was 15 years old, Therese joined Marie and Pauline in the convent at Lisieux. Here it was that Therese of the Child Jesus, the Little Flower as she called herself, bloomed with a sweet bright spirit for the nine years left of her life. She no longer had to fight the world to satisfy her will (which was now God's will). She had the *everything* she sought.

But she was still a fighter in the battle against herself. She set out to be a saint as deliberately as Joan of Arc set out to lead her army. She had always had an intense wish to be a Crusader or a missionary or, even better, a missionary martyr. She knew this was not to be. "Great deeds are not for me," she wrote. "I cannot preach the gospel or shed my blood. No matter. My brothers work in my stead, and I, a little child, stay close to the throne and love .... But how shall I show my love, since love proves itself by deeds? Well, the little child will strew flowers before Thee — that is, I will let no opportunity for sacrifice pass, no look, no work. I will make use of every little opportunity."

And she did. She did it so cheerfully, so quietly, hardly any of the sisters noticed her. When she was dying, the nuns shook their heads with pity and said what a shame it was that they couldn't find anything of importance to write about this little nun.

She did nothing unusual, nothing that would call attention to herself. She did the work given her, answered sharp remarks with kind ones, was friendly to those who were not. Her life was one of secret adventure, of giving to God a daily bouquet of offering up and giving in. No pinprick of annoyance was too small for Therese. She offered up being splashed by dirty laundry water with the same enthusiasm she offered up the cold.

She felt the cold deeply, right down into her bones. She would wrap herself in the thin blanket and shiver most of the night away in her damp room, but she would not ask for the comfort of another blanket. She would eat whatever was set before her, as is, whether the potatoes needed salt or the carrots were cooked to mush, and from the look on her face, you'd think it was apple pie and ice cream.

Therese likened her hidden life to that of the small white flower of springtime. She writes that when Jesus opened the book of nature to her, she saw that "every flower has a beauty of its own; that the splendor of the rose and the lily's whiteness do not deprive the violet of its scent . . . . So it is in the world of souls, the living garden of the Lord. It pleases him to create great saints, who may be compared with the lilies or the rose; but he has also created little ones, who must be content to be daisies or violets nestling at his feet . . . . Just as the sun shines equally on the cedar and the little flower, so the Divine Sun shines equally on everyone, great and small. . . .

"If a little flower could talk, it seems to me it would say what God has done for it quite simply and without concealment. It would not try to be humble by saying it was unattractive and without scent, that the sun had destroyed its freshness or the wind broken its stem, when all the time it knew it was quite the opposite."

Her sister, Pauline, who had become the Mother Superior of the convent, suspected that Therese was more than a simple, commonplace flower of a soul and ordered her to write the story of her life and of what Therese called her Little Way.

So, for the next 18 months, she sat on her stool every evening in her cold cell, writing and filling three large notebooks with this journal. She put down everything she felt would explain this Little Way and how we could all follow it.

"I want to seek a way to heaven, a new way, very short, very straight . . . , the way of trust and absolute selfsurrender . . . .

"I am a very little soul, who can only offer very little things to Our Lord. I have not the courage to look through books for beautiful prayers. I do as a child who has not yet learned to read — I just tell our Lord all that I want and he understands."

While she was writing this journal, the nuns discovered that Therese was dying from tuberculosis, a disease which few survived at that time. Sometimes she was so weak she could barely dip her pen into her inkwell, so she was allowed to finish her journal in pencil. When it was done, she called it *The Story of a Soul.*

Therese's mission was to show us that God is our loving Father, not a stern taskmaster who sits with a frown, watching for us to make a mistake so he can pounce on us. He does not lie in wait to punish us because we ate the last Girl Scout cookie in the jug and lied about it. No matter what we do, Therese tells us, he is waiting and willing to forgive us.

Each of us has a mission from God, and as we grow older, he lets us know what it is. We may become tree surgeons or clam diggers or violin makers, according to our gifts. In everything we do, however, we may follow Therese's Little Way to heaven. All we need do is choose everything for our Lord! We may pick up a pin or wear socks that don't match or not stuff an apple core under the couch cushion. We may eat baked beans that have dried up and taste like bullets. Nothing is too small for the Little Way!

In September of her 24th year, Therese left this world but

promised she would be back. "I have never given the good God anything but love, and it is with love he will repay. After my death, I will let fall a shower of roses. I will spend my heaven in doing good upon earth!"

So when you feel more like a dandelion gone to seed than a little white flower and you are certain someone has tied your shoelaces together as you try to find your way, don't give up! Pray to Therese and know that she will hear you.

Then open your heart and your hands to catch the petals!

Guardian Angels

October 2

nce upon a time, long before he made the world, God created pure spirits which he called angels. Their job was to praise him, to be his messengers and, the hardest job of all, to watch over all of us on earth once God made us.

They were smarter and more powerful than humans; they had to be if they were to be our guardians. God knew we would do a lot of stumbling trying to get to heaven, so he gave each of us our own special angel to guide and protect us along our way. Can you imagine all the millions of people running to and fro on the earth today, each with his own particular angel to steer him in the right direction?

Guardian angels are so marvelous to have around. We know that no matter what awful things lie before us or how frightened we are, we are never, ever alone. Right now, right there beside you, your angel stands ready to protect you from any danger.

Our angels not only defend us from harm to our bodies but also to our souls. As the psalmist sings, "He has given his angels charge over thee to keep thee in all thy ways." They help us to pray, to fight back when we are tempted. They warn us when to steer clear of people or places which will turn us away from our Lord. And their final job, after a lifetime of watching over us, is to lead us safely into heaven.

Only when they present us to God at his throne can they rest and enjoy heaven with us. We should be the best of friends, for no one

225

outside of God and Mary will ever know us as well as our own angel.

Sometimes we may see our angel, if he wishes us to, but more often it is enough that we simply feel his presence. He may take any shape he chooses. He may be a policeman we've never seen before who comes to our aid when we are lost in traffic. Or a very nice old lady in the market (whom we've never seen before) who returns the $5 bill we dropped on the floor. Or the nurse in the hospital who brings a drink of water during the night and who never appears again.

I know a mother who stood on the shore of an angry ocean, screaming for help as she watched her two little children being pulled out to sea by the undertow. Suddenly, a man appeared out of nowhere, a stranger. He ran past her, plunged fully clothed into the roaring waves, and grabbed the children just as they were at the crest of a wave that would have taken them beyond reach. He brought them, one in each arm, to their mother, who hugged them as if she would never let them go. When she turned to thank the man, he was gone. Disappeared, never to be seen again. She knows he was *somebody's* guardian angel.

St. Frances of Rome had an angel who came to her in the form of an eight-year-old boy. He visited with her and they sat and talked about things and he wrote her notes in gold lettering in her prayer book. She describes him: "His aspect is full of sweetness and majesty. Words cannot describe the divine purity of his gaze!"

Other saints have loved these companion angels too. Augustine taught that "the angels watch over us poor pilgrims. They have compassion on us and hasten to our aid at God's command. Go where we will, they are always with us."

And Jerome believed that "so sublime is the dignity of the soul that from its birth, there is appointed to each one a guardian spirit."

And Bernard told us to "Revere your guardian angel! Be grateful for the care he bestows on you! Have confidence in him, love him, and turn to him to entreat his protection in every difficulty, danger, and temptation! Make the holy angels your friends!"

There is a family I know with lots of noisy, scrapping

226

children who are always getting bumped and falling down stairs and tripping over dogs and shoelaces. Every morning when they dash out the door for the school bus, their mother says a prayer to their guardian angels so she won't worry about them during the day.

And at night, just before they go to bed, they say the same prayer for themselves and for all their friends who live far away:

> O Angel of God,
> My guardian dear,
> To whom God's love
> Commits me here,
> Ever this night,
> Be at my side,
> To light, to guard,
> To rule and guide.

Then, as they lie down on cool pillows, they never for a moment have to worry about burglars or bats or spooks who tug at the blankets or wolves that scratch at the door or spiders that come down from the ceiling in the dark and land in their hair.

Guardian angels are *such* a comfort!

Francis of Assisi

October 4

ave you ever wondered who is the patron saint of moles and cockroaches and three-toed sloths and lizards that sleep under rocks? Is there anyone who watches over cabbage moths and shamrocks and woolly bears who inch across a busy road? Does anyone give a hoot about the rowdy screech owl?

Of course someone does, and his name is Francis of Assisi. He called himself God's fool, Brother Ass and *Il Poverello,* the little poor man. But we call him the saint for everyone and everything. He loved every bit of the world God had created and said we were all part of one family with one Father. Wind and sun, gnats and fishes, fire and ice — all were his sisters and brothers. Nor would he close the door on pain or death, for they too were relatives in this family.

Francis really began his life as John, but because his father, Pietro Bernardone, traveled often to France and his mother was French, they nicknamed him *Il Francesco,* the little Frenchman, and from that came *Francis.* Pietro was a wealthy cloth merchant in the town of Assisi, and from the time he could walk, Francis loved to toddle about the shop, touching the bolts of velvet and lace and satins which the noble ladies came to buy. He could not wait until he could wear fine clothes from these goods and look every inch the dashing rich boy he was.

Francis spent his youth without a worry or care to make him frown. Every day was an adventure, every night a party that never stopped, filled with wine and pastries and loud joking and singing till the sky grew light. Francis was small and quick and cheerful as a sparrow — but a sparrow dressed in the finest of red velvet, wearing gold rings and chains and silver buckles on his shoes.

Whatever mischief was planned by the young men of the town, you can be sure Francis was the ringleader. He didn't care about work or school, nor did he think long, heavy thoughts about life. He just played, or he dashed about on his horse over the Umbrian hills, exulting in the great fun of living. He drank too much and sang too much, and he danced till there were holes in the soles of his shoes. Pietro and Pica, his mother, just shook their heads and smiled.

"Boys will be boys," his father shrugged. "Why shouldn't he enjoy himself? He's only young once! And why should he worry about working? We've got all the money he needs."

And the townspeople shook their heads and smiled. Yes, Francis was a rascal, but such a warm, loving rascal, you couldn't get angry with him. And he was so generous — he never refused anyone a request. He would grow up and become a soldier or a knight and that would straighten him out.

By the time he was 20, he had his first chance to act as a knight for his country. Assisi was part of the province of Umbria, and Umbria and its neighbor, Perugia, were always at war over something. Anything could start it. It could be something as small as the smell from a Perugian pig farm that wafted over to Umbria and curdled the milk. Whatever the reason, a war broke out between the two provinces and Francis was the first to jump on his horse to fight for the honor of Umbria.

Before he had time to get hurt, the young soldier was captured, along with his friends, and spent a year in a Perugian prison. Even in such a depressing spot, he kept up everyone's spirits with his foolishness. He told jokes that were so silly people had to laugh even as they groaned. He sang old drinking songs, dancing around the cell with a make-believe violin of two sticks tucked under his chin. He made funny faces behind the jailers' backs. Nothing could keep him down, and he marked off the days on the wall till he could go back to the good times awaiting him at home.

Then the war ended as suddenly as it began and Francis burst out of the prison, free at last. He walked toward home happily, quickly, breathing in the good Umbrian air. He wondered if his clothes would still be in style. No matter, his father could have the best tailor zip him up a new tunic and trousers in no time. Suddenly he stopped, his way blocked by a man in ragged, smelly clothes. The man, who was a beggar, simply sat in the middle of the road with open hands.

He looked up at Francis with sadness in his eyes. Francis did not want to meet a beggar today. It was too depressing, but his heart was too tender to allow him to pass by.

"Please, sir, could you spare some money so I might buy a coat to keep warm? Not an expensive one, but a little, cheap, thin one to keep the chill off." He looked at Francis and sighed. "I used to have a red velvet cape like yours, once, long ago ... when I was a knight."

Francis at once took off his clothes and tossed them to the shivering man. "Here, my friend, now give me yours so I can go home in style!" What a good joke it would be to arrive home like that! The beggar wanted to hug him but he didn't because he knew he was dirty and smelly. So Francis hugged *him,* and went on his way, whistling, to Assisi.

He went back to his old life, free to do and have everything he wanted. But something was wrong. All the old pleasures did not excite him. They seemed rather dull and childish now. He would leave parties to go out to look off into a sky full of stars, seeking he knew not what. His friends teased him. "What pretty girl are you dreaming of tonight, Francis?"

And one night he answered, very quietly, "A lovely one, more lovely and pure than I shall ever know again. Her name is Lady Poverty, and she shall be my bride."

This was certainly strange talk from someone who had never before been serious. His friends remembered that he had had a bout with a fever when he was in prison. Perhaps he hadn't recovered com-

pletely? But Francis was not feverish. He saw coolly and clearly the life ahead of him, and with all the joy he had given to his troubadour songs, he began his lifelong hymn to God.

One day when he was sitting in the Church of St. Damian wondering just how he would marry Lady Poverty, a voice coming from the crucifix on the wall said to him, "Francis, rebuild my house which is in ruins." Francis had no doubt that this was God telling him to repair the Church of St. Damian, which was old and crumbling and just about falling down.

So he went immediately to his father's store, took down several bolts of the finest satin, and sold them for a good deal of money. He ran with it to the pastor of St. Damian and gave it to him to repair the church, but the pastor didn't seem very happy about this great gift.

First of all, this young man was a bit strange. Where did he get so much money? Stole it most likely. The priest was just starting to say *no, thank you,* when the door burst open and there stood Francis' father, furious and with fists clenched. He grabbed Francis by the collar and shook him up and down. How dare he steal from his own father!

He dragged Francis home and locked him in his room until he would come to his senses and apologize. Pica, his gentle mother, came and begged him to do this so they could go back to being a happy family again. But Francis said he could not. "God told me to rebuild his church and I must obey him."

So his father brought him before the Bishop and the Church court to shame his son publicly. Pietro was hurting inside. All the high hopes he had for his son were dashed. His friends would think him a fool to be proud of such a one as Francis.

The Bishop listened to Pietro and then to Francis. Then the Bishop shook his head. "Francis, if you want to serve the Lord, you can't do it by stealing. You cannot use stolen money for the Lord; it has to be freely given."

Francis replied that from now on he would call only God his Father. He took off his fine silk blouse and velvet knickers, his dancing shoes and rings and chains and laid them at his father's feet. He stood naked in front of the Bishop and said now he owned nothing and owed nothing. The Bishop came down and wrapped his cloak around Francis' shoulders and embraced him. Pietro picked up the clothes and shoes and ornaments and walked away without a word. He no longer had a son.

Francis went off with a joy it is hard to describe. Now he was truly poor, like Christ, with absolutely nothing to his name but an old brown tunic that looked like a nightshirt, gathered in with a length of rope. He had no purse, no bread, no Bible, nothing but his absolute trust in God as a loving Father.

He was dancing a little jig down the road when a group of bandits saw him carrying on and decided to rob him. They thought he was probably drunk so they'd have an easy time taking whatever he had. They grabbed him and searched him up and down, then threw him into a ditch, disgusted because they found nothing. Francis was still singing.

"Keep quiet, you crazy loon," growled one of them, "or we'll give you something to howl about! Who are you anyway?"

Francis climbed up out of the ditch, rubbing away the blood from his scratches, and bowed low. "I am the herald of the King!" He laughed and continued his dance down the road.

He went back to St. Damian and, with the pastor's permission, he began to repair the old church by himself. He was as clever with his hands as he was with his mind, and the work he did with stone and wood and bricks was a pleasure to the eye.

One Sunday, when the work was done, he was listening to the Gospel and the words came into his heart and refused to budge:

"If you would be perfect, go and sell all you have and give it to the poor."

And, "Take nothing for your journey, neither purse nor bread, nor yet two coats nor staff."

And now he had an idea of what he was to do, what God had been trying to tell him. He was not to restore parish churches. He was to renew *the* Church.

So Francis went about preaching poverty and trust in God. It was very simple, so simple the people could not believe his message. He was called an impossible dunce, a vagabond, a leech who lived off other people. How dare he tell them that poverty was the one true way to Christ? Hadn't they been poor all their lives? And that love of God and one's neighbor was the only way to find peace? He was laughed at by people who were once his friends. His old neighbors scolded him for bringing such shame to his parents. And they threw rotten fruit and eggs and dead, disgusting things at him.

Francis wondered whether he had heard God right. Surely he would win no hearts here! But God answered him quickly. Before long a wealthy merchant, richer even than Francis' father, heard him preach and joined him. And then a priest, and then a woodcutter. Before long there were 12 of them, God's beggars, who went about preaching and begging for their food and sleeping on the ground or in caves at night.

One night Francis had a vision of hundreds of brothers in brown robes coming towards him and a voice saying to him, "I have chosen you to proclaim my Kingdom!" The next day, he went out and begged paper, ink and pen so he could set down the rules for his new order, which he would call the Friars Minor.

The Friars would, above all, trust in the Lord completely for all their needs. They would love all created things as their sisters and brothers. They would own nothing, not money, or land, or even a Bible. "If we own anything," Francis said, "we must have weapons to defend it, from which come quarrels and battles."

He rolled up his papers and took his Rule to Rome for the Pope's approval. The Pope was charmed by the little man with the dark, burning eyes, but he would not give his consent. He thought the Rule too strict, too hard. Why, sleeping on the ground like that, and not even owning a change of clothes! It was impossible to be that perfect.

But that night, *he* had a dream. He saw the great church of St. John Lateran falling, crumbling into dust, and only one ragged little man was holding it up. It was Francis. Our Lord said to the Pope, "This is the man through whom the Church shall be rebuilt.''

The next morning the Pope called Francis to him and gave him his blessing. The Friars Minor were now officially approved. (They were called Minor so they wouldn't be tempted to be Major, or greater than anyone else.)

The order grew and grew, just as Francis had seen in his vision, and the brothers' influence on the people who listened to them was great. Soon the brothers went out of Italy; two by two they preached missions all over Europe. And everywhere they went, people listened.

And when Francis spoke, *all* his brothers and sisters hung on to his every word. The animals were as close to him as his human brothers. They sat quietly as he told them stories of our Lord's love for them and why they each had special colors or markings. He called the crested lark Brother Friar because he was dressed in a brown habit and hood. He told the robin that her breast was red because when she came to comfort our Lord on the cross, she pricked herself on his thorny crown.

And the frightened brown rabbit that nestled in his arms was comforted by his promise that her fur would turn white by the time the first snow fell, so she would be safe from foxes and hunters.

He had a way with larger animals too, especially a very large, angry, ferocious, ravenous wolf. This wolf had frightened the people in the town of Gubbio half to death. And those he didn't frighten to death, he ate. For some time, he made a habit of eating a person a day.

The terrified people thought he was a savage beast who ate them out of hatefulness. They never stopped to think that wolves get hungry, too. But the wolf and the people never got close enough to each other to try to talk things over.

When Francis came to Gubbio to see if he could talk to the wolf, the people had locked themselves in their homes. They peered out from behind curtains to watch this little man, who was brave but certainly not very bright.

Suddenly the hated wolf sprung out from behind a gooseberry bush. He was snarling and hissing and foaming at the mouth and had

the wildest red eyes and yellow fangs Francis had ever seen. Just as he was about to land on Francis and probably crush him, Francis called out, "Brother Wolf! Stop right this moment and hear God's Word!" And he quickly made the Sign of the Cross over the beast.

The wolf fell in a heap at the little man's feet and began whimpering. Francis saw that his ribs showed through his skin, like bars on a cage, and that the hair of his tail was scraggly and flat, as if it didn't have the strength to stand up even in anger.

"Brother Wolf," said Francis as sternly as possible (which wasn't very stern at all), "I command you, in our Lord's name, never to eat anyone again! Or do any harm to this town, ever. It's your town, too, you know. And you're not to knock over garbage pails or bite the heads off tulips when you feel out of sorts. Do you promise?"

The wolf hung his head and said nothing.

"Why have you done all these awful things?" asked Francis.

"I was hungry," sobbed the wolf. "All night long, I couldn't sleep because my stomach growled and kept me awake. Then I went out looking for food to keep my stomach quiet—nuts, berries, bark, *anything*—but there was nothing. One week all I had was an old shoe and a bunch of thistles, and thistles are very bad on your throat. Then I ate a little boy's hat and that wasn't bad, so I went back and ate the little boy. And then my stomach didn't growl."

So Francis told him how wrong this was, that no one could take the life of another, even if all he had to eat was thistles. He told him that God loved him and would see to it that he'd never be hungry again, and that the good people of Gubbio would feed him every day if he promised never to harm them.

So the wolf promised and gave Francis his paw to seal the promise. And from that time on, the wolf was like a big pet dog. He even let the children ride on him.

Of all the creatures, the birds were Francis' pets. Whenever he preached, they would gather and crowd the trees and towers and chimneys. Larks and linnets and turtle doves and yellow-bellied sapsuckers and chickadees and sea gulls — they would twitter and chirp and warble and shriek, until their song drowned out Francis' words. Once they made such a racket Francis had to ask them please to be quiet.

"Sister birds, you have had your say, now please let me have mine. My word is from God and it is for you, too, to hear." So they quietly lowered their beaks, hid their heads in their wings, and not a whisper was heard until Francis was finished. And *then* were they loud!

On the evening Francis died, a gathering of larks swelled overhead and dipped and soared and sang their hearts out in their grief over losing him. Francis, who lay naked on his Sister Earth, smiled and whispered weakly, "My sweet sisters! No angel choir could pierce my heart as does your song. When I can no longer hear it, I know I shall be in heaven!"

And then they flew closer to one another and formed a cross of fluttering brown wings. They soared higher and higher, until the cross was but a pinprick in the heavens, and their song as faint as a child singing himself to sleep.

When the song of the larks could no longer be heard, the body of Francis lay still on the earth. His sisters had brought their brother home, and what excitement this caused in heaven.

You wouldn't believe that party! Honey and almond cakes (Francis' favorite) and pistachio ice cream and cherry soda — enough for everyone in heaven. (Since people in heaven do not make pigs of themselves, there is always enough.)

Then a cricket hopped out of Francis' pocket and began to fiddle a dance. And Francis jumped up, all glowing and smiling as when he was a boy, and danced and sang and fiddled in his foolish joy — and this time he had a *real* violin.

Back on earth, the brown rabbit who would soon grow white and hide in the snow heard the commotion and twitched her whiskers with delight. She thumped out her message to those on earth and above and below:

"Francis is home, alive and well!"

Hedwig

October 16

O nce upon a time, there was a slip of a girl named Hedwig who was born into a royal family in Bavaria. Everyone exclaimed over the beauty of this child, whom God had fashioned as delicately as a china figurine. Her mother called her "my golden girl," and Hedwig was truly as warm and bright as a sudden shaft of sunlight shining through the window on a winter's afternoon.

She gave her parents no problems at all. She sat patiently as servants wove ribbons through her golden braids. She sipped her tea without ever making a noise. She was every inch the young countess of the castle and might have been that forever, had God not decided otherwise.

For six years she lived as the loved and loving child of Count Berthold and his wife, and then her parents took her to live at a nearby monastery in Kissingen. Here she would learn everything she would need to know as the future wife of a count or prince or whomever her parents would choose for her. She was taught to play the harp and embroider with pearls and paint flowers on china plates, and she could plan a banquet for a hundred princes and their wives without getting flustered. Here also she grew in her love for God. She wished in her heart that she might stay here forever, to love and serve him quietly and never go back to the world again.

But our Lord told Hedwig he had other plans for her. She

waited patiently for him to explain, all the while she was sewing and lettering and learning to make tea from herbs. Then, when she was 12 years old, he did. Her father brought her the news that she was to be the wife of Prince Henry, the son of his good friend Boleslav the Tall of Silesia, which was in the far-off land of Poland.

Hedwig was shaken and sad, but she tried not to let her feelings show. (It wouldn't have done her any good even if she had, because in those days, marriages were arranged by parents, often before their children were born. Sometimes this was a sad situation. The brides and grooms, often very young, had no choice but to make the best of it. So for the glory of God, country and family, they married people they had never met and often didn't like when they did.)

But Henry and Hedwig felt their marriage was truly made in heaven (which, of course, it was). From the moment they met on their wedding day, they knew they would never love anyone else as they did each other. Even the sorrow of packing and leaving her family to live in a strange land was not as strong as Hedwig's desire to be the perfect wife for Henry.

As for the Prince, he soon discovered that his bride was as inquisitive as she was beautiful. She wanted to know everything about everything in her new home. She began asking questions from the moment she set foot in the royal carriage that would take them to Silesia. Why was there so much snow? Why were there so many prisons and no hospitals? How do you make beet soup? Why did the peasants never smile?

And when Henry replied it was because they were poor and hungry, Hedwig would ask *why* they were poor and hungry.

Henry smiled and answered that it was not for her to be concerned. She was his wife, a mere woman, and was not to think of unpleasant things. But he soon discovered that Hedwig had too quick a mind to forget what she saw. Her desire to know the *why* and *how* of everything made Henry look for the answers himself.

He began to ask her advice on all sorts of things, about taxes and gold mines and hunting bear and growing buckwheat. Hedwig always seemed to know how to solve a prickly problem. With a nod or touch or gentle questioning, she helped guide his heart to the right solution:

"Free these prisoners so they may see God's love through you!"

"Look at those little children shivering together. They must have wool coats and caps and mittens to keep warm, and boots lined with fur so their toes will not freeze!"

"My husband, the mothers need rye bread and sour cream and fresh eggs. Surely once a week you can share our bounty with them!"

Quietly, like drops of rain that will not cease, her desire to help her people wore through Henry's indifference. He began to see they had equal claim with him to God's love. Hedwig reminded him whenever he tired of doing good, "You know, Henry, but for the grace of God, *you* could be the thief in prison and I could be the mother with nothing to feed her babe. We are who we are for a reason."

And so, despite himself, Henry became a ruler who truly cared about his people. And he was the first to admit it was because of Hedwig. He loved his wife more than life itself and could not bear to say no to her requests, even if he didn't agree about their importance. When he would see a certain sweetly-determined look in her eye as they talked at breakfast, he would sigh and pretend to groan.

"Now what, my little Jadwiga! You want flannel underwear for all the servants because it is drafty in the castle? Such nonsense! It's good for them to be cold. It builds their character and keeps them humble. But all right, all right, they shall have it of course. Just don't look at me with those sad eyes."

By the time she was 26, Hedwig had six children. They were quarrelsome, and she had her hands full trying to teach them to love one another and not fight every moment of the day. Sometimes she thought they stopped only when they ate, and even then they would throw their mashed potatoes in a fit of temper.

Whenever she had a free moment away from the children,

Hedwig continued to try to make life easier for her people. She felt that the time had come to build the country's first monastery school for women. Women who could not read or write were not a blessing to anyone, she told Henry. She wanted them to learn these things and then study astronomy and medicine and music. Then they could go and teach others as they had been taught.

Henry said, "Absolutely not!" The country could not afford such a luxury, women did not need to read or write, and that was that.

Hedwig gave the matter back to God. "Please, Lord," she prayed, "you put this idea into my head. Now please help me to make it come true."

The next day Henry decided they should all go hunting in the great forest. It was the first time he had refused his wife anything and he wanted to make it up to her. So off they went, Henry and Hedwig and their servants, dressed in furs and scarlet robes.

Henry galloped ahead to clear a path — and he found himself on a road which was not known to him. The ancient oaks seem to close in on him and the path became as narrow as a foot trail in the woods. Suddenly, the ground beneath Henry's horse became soft and the horse swiftly began to sink. No matter how he struggled, Henry could not pull the horse out of the mucky marsh. Up to his knees in mud, Henry realized in a flash that not all the gold in his treasury could save him now. What good was his money, his power!

He remembered his wife's pleading for a women's monastery and called out to God, "My Lord, help me get out of this, and upon my return, I shall build your women a marvelous, incredible monastery!"

And the horse sprung forward as if the angels had lifted him and cleared the mud. He carried the weary prince back to Hedwig, who already knew what had happened before Henry told her.

And so the monastery at Trebnitz was built with the help of all the prisoners Henry freed in exchange for their work. As the years passed, monasteries and hospitals popped up wherever there was a need. It would seem that this would be enough to keep the royal couple busy, but this is just what they did when they were *relaxing*.

Most of their energy went into surviving wars. It was a time when wars were as expected as snow in winter. There were wars to keep out savage invaders, wars among the ruling princes of Poland, even wars between their own sons when they grew up and began fighting in earnest.

One enemy who constantly worried Henry was Swatopluk of Pomerania. Henry and Hedwig could not lay their heads down and rest easy, for they never know when the wily leader would strike.

With great cunning, Swatopluk once chose the moment when Henry was helpless in his bath to rush in and slash him with his sword. This made Henry furious. Despite his bleeding wound, he jumped out and chased the scoundrel into the hills without even grabbing a towel. Henry escaped with his life — barely.

Hedwig brought herbs and ointment for his cut and brewed tea with lemon and whiskey to cure his shivers. But as soon as he took a few sips, he had to get dressed and be off to fight yet another enemy, Conrad of Plock, who was every bit as mean as Swatopluk.

With God's help, Henry defeated Conrad and set up his new kingdom at Krakow. While he was at Mass giving thanks, Conrad crept in and captured him, tied him up, and carried him off.

When Hedwig heard about this, she put on her gray cloak and followed her husband. With her gentle persuasion, she coaxed the two angry men to come to peace with each other.

"For shame," she said, "you are both Poles; why do you fight each other? And Conrad, I have good news for you. We would like your daughters to marry our sons! Now is this any way to give them a good start?" The men listened and agreed and from that time on treated each other as friendly relatives. Hedwig thanked the Lord that she had been able to stop a little killing for a little while.

The years passed and the children grew up and moved away. Hedwig and Henry realized they had grown old. Soon, they knew, their love story on earth would be over, but they were not sad. They knew the best was yet to come — a brand new life in heaven!

When Henry died, the nuns at the monastery of Trebnitz

cried and cried. But Hedwig sat quietly with dry eyes and kept knitting mittens from odd bits of yarn. She comforted the nuns.

"Why are you crying, dear sisters? Our lives are God's. He puts us here for his own reasons and, when our work is done, we go on to do other work. When the bread is baked, we take it out of the oven, don't we? Come, let us rejoice. Dear Henry is stirring things up in heaven!"

Hedwig lived the rest of her life with the sisters at Trebnitz but did not become a nun. She kept the freedom of a royal princess so she could go out and continue to nurse the sick and work with the poor. Her son, Henry the Good, became king and continued to fight the invaders of Poland as his father had.

One day, as she used up the last bits of yarn in a pair of baby bootees, she called the sisters to her and said it was time for her to leave them and would they please call the priest.

They told her she was silly for she was in the best of health. "No," she said, "I want him *now.*" So the priest came and when he touched her forehead with the oil, Hedwig smiled. "Look," she called out excitedly, "don't you see them? A whole procession of angels is coming in!"

And a great light shone about her head, as dazzling as a crown of diamonds catching the sun. Jadwiga, the little Lily of Poland, left with her heavenly escort to join her waiting husband. They met in a celebration that went on and on and on for *days.*

Hedwig said it was better than a Polish wedding.

All Saints' Day

November 1

ome out, come out
Wherever you are!
In bed or boat
Or under the car,
Planting a lily,
Braiding a rug,
Stirring up chili,
Dissecting a bug,
Milking a cow,
Stuffing a pillow,
Extolling a star,
Stripping a willow —
Come out, come out
From near and far!

For today is the day,
The first of November,
To celebrate saints
You may not remember.
The Big Ones you know,
They stand quite tall,
Like Francis and Vincent

247

And Peter and Paul,
But in their shadow
The unknowns cluster,
Loved by God
As a hot dog its mustard.

This is the day our Father has made
For Crispin and Nestor and sweet Adelaide,
And Wiltrudia and Finnian and Adalbert and Emma,
And Audrey and Priscilla and Paphnutius and Otto,
And Zachary and Flora and Isaac of Cordova,
And Winifred and Poppo and Blessed Rizzerio.

This is the day the King has given
To Meinrad and Thecla and Bruno and Swithin,
To Olaf of Norway,
And Eric of Sweden,
Mechtilde of Hackeborn,
And Simeon, Armenian,
To Trumwin and Jutta and Hilda and Chad,
And Dymphna and Botwid and Ethelnoth and Gall,
To Gerlac and Munchin, Nutburga and Narcissus,
Who served him on earth, who gave him their all.

This is the day our Lord decrees
Diadem and doves and gifts that will please
To Ptolemy and Englebert, Modwenna and Canute,
And Ida of Toggenberg and Gertrudia of Delft,
And Blessed Thomas Plumtree and Josephat of Plotsk,
And Oswald of Northumbria and little John the Dwarf.

Come out, come out,
And stand in the sun!
For this is the day for all holy ones,

For saints true-tested and those not done
Who live right now, daughters and sons:

The man with warts who trims your tree,
The librarian who stamps your books,
And Alice Gray, who sings sad songs,
And the lady in school who cooks,

The teacher who gives you too much homework,
The priest who is fat and sweaty,
Your cousin who always does everything better,
The clown who throws confetti.

Come out, come out,
Bake cakes or trout!
Come, sit down and rest awhile,
Adjust your crown and royal smile,
Curl your hair, make a fuss —
This is the day for *all* of us!

Martin de Porres

November 3

nce upon a time, there was a saint who could fly through the air faster than a bird, a passing bullet, or the speed of light. He wasn't Superman or even Supersaint. He was Martin de Porres.

Martin wasn't a saint because he could fly, and he didn't fly because he was a saint. Flying, or *teleporting,* was only one of the incredible gifts which God had given him. These were spectacular, eye-popping, now-watch-this-one gifts, like fireworks that bring forth ooooh's and aaaah's as they burst upon the sky.

Our Lord, with his divine sense of humor, chose someone you'd least expect to perform his magic, a sweet, humble man who would have been just as happy sweeping floors or saving mice. His name was Martin de Porres and he was born in Lima, Peru, in the 16th century. Like Rose of Lima, who lived at the same time and was his friend, he knew from childhood that all he wanted to do with his life was give it to the Lord.

And, like Rose, he was the son of a Spanish aristocrat. Unlike Rose, he was a *mulatto,* which means that one of his parents was white and the other black. Their way of life was different from birth. Yet, through their love for a God who knew no differences, Martin and Rose were drawn together as friends.

Martin was the natural son (which means his parents were

not married) of Juan de Porres, a Spanish knight, and Anna, a black woman who had come to Peru from Panama. After Martin's sister Juana was born, his father went away and left Anna to take care of herself and the children as best she could.

It was a struggle to make ends meet. Anna took in wash and Martin and Juana, little as they were, helped her scrub the bags of dirty laundry left by the Spaniards. The children had a sweet and sunny outlook, with no trace of resentment against those who had more than they (which was practically everyone). Martin was at times too generous, as far as his mother was concerned. He would exasperate her by giving away the money she gave him to buy food at the market or, if he got as far as the market to buy it, by giving the food away to beggars. He could not resist a tearful eye or quivering lip. Even chickens followed him home, knowing they would get the last of the corn or crumbs.

When Martin was 12, his father sent money to Anna to give the children an education. She apprenticed Martin to a barber because he had already shown a gift for healing. In those days, a barber was also a surgeon who sewed up cuts, set bones, cured fevers and applied poultices to wounds to draw out infections. So if you fell out of a tree and broke your arm the day you needed a haircut, you could take care of both at the same shop.

Martin loved this work. He woke each morning with excitement, wondering what good he would do with his hands and skill that day. He was satisfied that he would spend his life curing all those who came to him. This would be his work for God.

But God told Martin he wanted more. One night, as he lay weary and happy on his cot in the barbershop, God woke him. "Martin," he whispered, "I want you to use your gifts for helping others, but first I want you to serve me with prayer and penance."

Martin understood. And his mother and sister understood. He said good-bye to them (but not forever since they would still be in the same town) and went off to the Dominican monastery of the Holy Rosary. Here he knew his life would be centered around God from dawn to dark. He asked the monks if he might join them, not as a priest or a brother, but as a servant of all of them. He wanted to be a *donado,* one who gives himself completely to God in the service of others.

The Prior was delighted to accept this young boy (he was just 15) whose healing skill was already well-known to him. Martin's father, Juan, who had come back to Lima on a visit, was quite annoyed. Even though he didn't actually want to *be* Martin's father—after all, the boy had skin the color of coffee with cream—he expected the boy to remember his noble origin.

"The least you could do," he sniffed, "is become a priest, not a servant."

But Martin knew what he was doing. He didn't want the comfort or high esteem of being a priest. He wanted to take on the lowliest tasks, and he did. He swept and scoured and made beds and cleaned out garbage pails and stables. He washed the altar linens and the brothers' habits. He gathered herbs and flowers for ointments and teas. In short, he did anything he was asked.

Lima had been taken over by Spanish conquerors such as Martin's father. Even though they had killed the natives and had stolen their land and gold, they considered themselves good Christians. They did not see themselves as they really were—cruel, selfish and un-Christlike. Instead, they painted pictures of themselves inside their minds as generous men of God. So to balance the evil they did, they gave huge amounts of money to be used for the poor.

And his superiors asked Martin to take care of seeing that everyone got a fair share. It was hard to find an honest man in those days, but Martin had become known as a completely honest person in handling money, one who would never keep anything for himself. Because he always said yes, Martin was quick to put his broom away and go forth to work with the poor, whom he had always loved.

Every week he used every bit of $2,000 for food and medicine and clothing. He gave it to poor boys who wished to become priests and to poor girls who wanted to marry or enter a convent. He used it to found an orphanage and to free prisoners. And if he had any pennies left over, he bought very ripe bananas so the baker at the monastery could make a treat of banana bread.

While he was taking care of the poor outside the monastery, he was still taking care of the aches and pains of the monks within. Because he could heal so quickly and naturally, the word spread into the town about the wonder-worker who cured with a touch of his hand. Each day, more and more people waited at the door of the infirmary, clamoring to see Martin. It began to look like a large city clinic, with long lines of people coming and going all day long.

The monks began to complain. It wasn't healthy having all these sick people coming to the monastery, they said. So Martin's sister Juana, who had a home of her own by now, opened her doors to them. She must have been as generous and loving as her brother. We know very little about her, but I wouldn't doubt that she is a saint, too.

Martin's gift of healing gave much glory to God but it also gave Martin a headache. He had chosen to live the hidden life of a *donado,* trying to be the least among men. Yet he had been given these extraordinary gifts. He didn't ask for them and maybe he really didn't want them—but he had them! There was no way out but to use them and to hold nothing back.

He used his natural skill and learning first and gave them the credit for his cures. But in his heart he knew that it was often just his touch that did it. In such cases, he would make a joke or it or give some simple remedy as the cure, treating it lightly.

Once he treated the Governor of Mexico for a very sore throat with a high fever. He was cured immediately by drinking the medicine which Martin had given him. It was just plain water! And another time, when a woman who was at death's door was healed, Martin said it was because she had eaten an apple as he had told her. (Maybe that's how we got the saying, "An apple a day keeps the doctor away." Well, it *could* be.)

Most of his cures occurred right within the monastery. Once there was a monk who had a fever for so long, it depressed him. The corner of his mouth turned down and he rolled his eyes and wore a long face which seemed to go on forever.

"I shall never get well," he moaned to Martin.

"Now, Brother," smiled Martin gently, "if you keep on saying that, you won't let yourself." Martin believed that being hopeful and of good cheer was the best part of a remedy, so he tried to coax people out of feeling sorry for themselves.

He told the monk to take a bath in the monastery pond when night fell and he would feel much better.

"Is that all?" asked the monk, a bit disappointed at such simple medicine.

"That will do it," said Martin.

So the monk shrugged his shoulders and made his way to the pond that night. It was a very strange cure, he thought, but since he was probably going to die anyway, he'd try it.

He jumped into the pool but the water was so cold, he lost his breath and jumped back onto the grass. Then he was so cold he jumped back in. This time he stayed in so long he almost froze and got so numb he couldn't climb out. A brother happened to pass by and pulled him out and wrapped him in warm blankets. He fell asleep immediately and when he woke the next morning, he found he wasn't dead. As a matter of fact, he felt marvelous and ready for a huge breakfast. He was never sick again!

Martin's compassion for the animals who were part of God's family was as great as that for humans. He felt especially concerned for rats and mice because, he said, the poor little things weren't as lovable as cats and dogs. And he couldn't convince his brother monks not to set traps for them.

"They are nothing but pests, Brother Martin, vermin!"

To make matters worse, the mice had invaded the vestry and were making lacework of the vestments with their sharp teeth. One angry monk exploded, "How would you like to say Mass with your cassock full of holes?"

Martin could understand their impatience but still he could not bear to kill or even scold his scurrying, squeaking friends.

He came to them that evening as they were busily shredding

the edges of a surplice. "My little brothers," he said gently, "you had better stop this mischief or you shall find yourselves caught in a trap and that will be the end of it. I can't protect you forever. Now, all of you, listen to me. Leave the monastery and go out to the garden, and I promise I will bring you food every day. It should be more enjoyable than this piece of cloth. Go, right now!" X *end -6 3'5*

And they did, every single one of them, as fast as you could blink an eye. They never again touched anything belonging to the church, and to the end of his days, Martin fed his mice in the garden.

It wasn't just mice who were charmed by his love. All animals obeyed him instantly. If you've ever tried to train your dog not to sleep on the couch, you know that it takes much patience and time to get animals to do what you want. But Martin had a special way with them. Chickens danced about his feet, mules and dogs and cats rubbed against him and thrust their heads into his hands so he could scratch behind their ears. He coaxed a mouse to eat from the same bowl as a cat and dog, and from that time on, they were all the best of friends.

The hospital at his sister's house soon included animal patients and a shelter for dogs and cats waiting to find homes. (Now I am sure Juana was a saint!)

One of the many stories about Martin and his animal friends is about a very old dog who belonged to the monk in charge of the kitchen at the monastery. This dog was very ancient—at least 18 years old—very slow, very clumsy with age. He had just about everything wrong with him, including a bad case of mange. He scratched and snuffled and wheezed and limped and, worst of all, he smelled. He smelled so bad the monks held their noses when he shuffled by, as if they had just smelled a skunk.

His owner decided sadly that he could no longer ask his brothers to put up with this, so he ordered the dog to be killed. While the dog stretched out in the sunshine, enjoying a nap, a servant threw a huge rock at the dog's head and killed him instantly. He was about to pick up the dog to throw him into the river when Martin stopped him.

He took the poor mangy, smelly animal into his arms and

carried him into his room. No sooner did the dog touch the floor than he pulled himself up, put his nose into Martin's hand, and tried to move his head back and forth. Martin cleaned the wound and sewed up the skin and then poured wine over it. The dog became dizzy from it and lay down and slept.

The next morning Martin brought him a bit of meat, and he sniffed at it then gulped it down. He wagged his tail, slipped through Martin's legs and ran off, completely cured—of *everything*. He smelled as clean as wash blowing dry in the wind. And he never again had to fear for his life.

All of these gifts would be enough to spread over a dozen saints, but Martin had even more startling ones. For one thing, he had the ability to rise in the air and stay there. He would sometimes become so rapt in his love for our Lord, the love would take over his body and make it light as a feather and bright as the sun. While at prayers he would often soar to the ceiling in the chapel or in his room. Once when a young novice was sent to find Brother Martin, he saw a brilliant light coming out from under the door to his room. He opened the door cautiously. Martin, who had risen off the floor, caught his foot in the novice's hood and nearly scared him out of his habit. It took quite a while for Martin to calm him down and help him realize this was nothing out of the ordinary.

For another thing, Martin could read minds. He often did this while cutting the hair of his brother monks. He would tell them gently that he knew what was troubling them (even if they always smiled and never admitted they were troubled) and give them the exactly right advice they needed. He could foretell the future. He knew who would leave the monastery and who would get up in the night and take food from the kitchen and who would sleep while they were supposed to be praying. He could even track down missing letters or people.

Once two novices disappeared. While he was praying, Martin read their minds (even though they were in another town). He whisked himself off and appeared to them through their locked doors. Once their fright wore off, he talked with them and told them that they really were meant to be monks; they were just tired and unsure right now. He put his arm around them and, in the wink of an eye, they were back at the monastery without anyone else ever knowing of it.

He had the gift of entering and leaving locked doors or barred windows without being seen. He walked through walls. Whenever he was needed, he was there, as if he had some special antenna that signaled an emergency. This ability led into an even more incredible gift—the gift of bilocation, which means that he could be in two places at one time. Now this sounds impossible. You know it's impossible because even your mother says, when three of you are yelling for her at once, "Will you please wait a minute, I can't be in two places at one time!"

But Martin could. While people saw him busy at work in Lima, he was traveling all over the globe, learning about new medicines in France, soothing the wounds of black slaves in Algeria, helping persecuted Christians in China and Japan. Wherever he was needed, he appeared.

You may think what fun you'd have if you had such powers! Why, you could eat hot dogs at a ball game in Baltimore or have the best seat in the house to see *The Nutcracker* ballet in New York. Or you could land in an ice cream factory and sample every single flavor until you got sick. And if you were sent to your room to study, you could always just fly out of the window and go to watch the changing of the guard at Buckingham Palace. The things you could do!

But Martin didn't do that. Whatever powers God gave Martin—the gifts of healing or reading minds or telling the future or raising the dead or flying through space—they were used only to bring glory to God. He did this so well he could be the patron saint of just about everyone. Barbers and beggars and pilots and locksmiths and magicians and nurses and veterinarians and old dogs and people with rats in their cellars and squirrels in their attics. He was like a jewel in the sun, giving off brilliance no matter how the rays caught it.

Yet whenever you see a picture of Martin, he is not doing anything as spectacular as flying through the air or walking through walls. You will see him with a broom in his hands and a mouse or two playing about his feet. This is the truest and most important picture, for it shows him as all he ever wanted to be—God's *donado*.

Now that he's in heaven, I wonder if Martin ever makes flying trips to earth when he's especially needed. Has any of you ever seen him?

Well, if ever I see someone in a black and white habit zooming across the sky, *I* won't be surprised. I'll know it's not an unidentified flying object. It's just Martin answering a call.

Frances Xavier Cabrini

November 13

nce upon a time, not very long ago, there lived a little girl named Mary Francesca who wanted to be a missionary to China more than anything else in the world. She would sit by a stream near her home and make boats out of empty pea pods. Then she would fill them with violets and pretend they were priests and nuns setting off on the journey to the East. Someday, she said, *she* would be doing that for real!

Mary Francesca, or Frances, was the 13th child born to a farming family in Lodi, Italy. You might think that the baby in such a large family would be terribly spoiled and determined to have her own way, but Frances was neither. Her sisters were quite strict and made her mind. (Anyone with many big brothers and sisters knows it is very hard to be spoiled with *them* around.)

At night, the family would read aloud from a book about the lives of the missionaries, and Frances thought again that this was exactly what she wanted to be. She practiced giving up candy and apricot pastries because she knew there would be nothing of that sort in China, so she had better get used to it. She wondered if she would have to eat raw fish when she got to China and prayed that if she did, God would give her the courage to swallow it quickly.

The years passed and young Frances grew up and became a teacher. She enjoyed this work but didn't feel it was enough to satisfy all

she wanted to do. Only working for God would do that.

Frances felt it was time to announce that she wanted to become a nun, and a missionary at that. She went to the Bishop and asked him if she might become a missionary and go to China.

"You want to join a missionary order?" he asked, with a slight frown. "Very well. I don't know of any, so go found one yourself."

Frances, who was very determined, set about doing just that. She, and seven young women as filled with grace and enthusiasm as she was, formed a society called the Missionary Sisters of the Sacred Heart. It wasn't a great success at first. Many people felt it just wasn't right for young women to be missionaries and to go off into strange lands. Frances would remind them that there is neither male nor female in the Lord and that all are equal in his sight.

Her good works in Italy soon won them over. Within a few years the sisters had set up schools for girls, homes for orphans, hotels for college students. Soon she opened two houses in Rome — a free school and a children's home.

One particular Bishop had been watching her and asked her to come see him. She did, wondering what was on his mind.

"Sister Frances," he began, "I have had my eye on you. I have in mind a missionary work of great importance for only the bravest, most determined believer in miracles. I believe you are the person God has in mind for me to send overseas!"

Frances was so excited her head spun. China, at last! She would sail to the Far East, not in a pea pod boat but in a real one.

"Frances," the Bishop said, "I want you to go to a foreign land — the United States, to work among our Italian people in New York City."

"Oh, no, thank you!" said Frances. She knew God wanted her to go to China, *not* New York City.

"But," he continued, "our people need you. They have so few priests to help them. They left here to find a new and better life for themselves. They thought they would never be poor or hungry again. Now, what do they find? They are ignored, pushed around, made fun of;

they work in sweatshops and dirty streets. They are still poor and hungry, and they are losing their faith besides.''

"No, thank you,'' she repeated, feeling a bit guilty.

The next day she received a letter from the Archbishop of New York, asking her please to come. And that night she had a dream in which the Pope came to her and said, "Not to the East, Frances, but to the West.''

There was no question now. Frances went to the Bishop and said yes. Once she made up her mind to something, she went full steam ahead. She packed her bags and gathered six of her strongest (in body and spirit) sisters and together they set off on their voyage west.

When they arrived in New York City, they found no one to meet them and no place to go. They stopped at the nearest hotel, which looked very down-at-the-heels with cracked shades and missing window panes. All of them stayed in one room. It was so dirty, they didn't want to turn on the light.

When they did, they heard the scurrying of hundreds of cockroaches disappearing into the woodwork. Rats — or maybe very big mice — hurried softly and quickly up and down the inside walls. The sisters did not want to pull down the bedsheets for fear of what they might find, so they spent the night kneeling and praying for courage to meet whatever tomorrow would bring.

The next day the Archbishop came to them and said he was sorry but the plans had been changed. There was no longer a building for them, so perhaps they had better go back to Italy.

Frances answered before his words died on the air. "The Pope sent me here and here I stay.'' He was taken aback by this spunky little woman who seemed to fear no one and who believed that nothing was impossible.

The sisters went to work. First, after finding a small home for themselves where their people lived in a part of New York called Little Italy, they learned the English language. They found a nearby building which they used to take in orphans or whatever children needed a home. When they needed money, they went out to beg. They went from door to door and shop to shop, and even to the police stations. They would take anything — food, clothing, money — and it was always just what they needed at the moment.

Frances taught her sisters that the poor did not depend on their small works but rather upon God's working through them. She told them to "pray always and ask without ceasing, that is, have your mind always fixed on prayer, and will only what God wills." And, she urged, "Have faith and you will behold miracles!"

She proved those words in her life. She traveled up and down this country, from Chicago to New Orleans, from Scranton to Denver, starting hospitals and schools and homes. She went to Central America and crossed the Andes Mountains on a mule. She crossed the ocean 30 times altogether to spread her work throughout England, France, Spain — and, yes, Italy.

When she was 59 years old, she became a citizen of the United States. She loved this land which had become her second home and which she now knew almost better than people born here. Many of you of Italian descent may have had grandparents or great-grandparents who remember the little nun who brought comfort and the strength to keep going to her people all over this country.

She is our first American saint and is buried under the altar of Mother Cabrini High School in New York City.

Mary Francesca did not fulfill her childhood dream of sailing off to China to win souls. But neither did her patron saint, Francis Xavier, who died within sight of its shore.

God had other plans for them. So they discarded theirs and followed his, and that's all any of us have to do to become saints.

Francis Xavier

December 3

nce upon a time, a young Spanish nobleman named Francis Xavier dreamed of becoming a famous scholar and philosopher. He would become so well-known that people on the street would whisper and shove and curtsy as he passed by and say to each other, "Look, there goes Francis Xavier, the well-known, handsome, talented, charming scholar whose books are in *all* the libraries of Spain!"

To make this dream come true, he knew he would have to study with all the brains God had given him, and that he did. He went to the University of Paris where he quickly became one of its best students. Here he met a strange man who was very unlike Francis (who *was* handsome, talented, charming, and on his way to becoming well-known). This man, whose name was Ignatius, was a former soldier, older, lame, uncaring as to how he looked (Francis was very fussy about his clothes).

Ignatius would wait in the shadows of the buildings, his stern eyes set in an unsmiling face, and when Francis passed by, he would whisper to him, "Psst! Francis! What does it profit a man if he gains the whole world and loses his soul?"

Not just once, but over and over he did this, until Francis became quite angry. He was upset and did not know why. The words stuck in his mind and would spring out at him when he didn't expect them. They haunted him, until one day he went to Ignatius and said, "I know you are a holy man and that God is speaking through you to me—but what do you want of me?"

Ignatius told him that he was forming an order of priests called the Society of Jesus and he had chosen Francis to be one of the first seven founders. Francis understood. "Well," he said, "this is one way for you to make sure I don't lose my soul!"

He began to study twice as hard now; and by the time he was 31 years old, he was ordained a priest. He went to Rome to work as Ignatius' letter-writer, so he was the first to open and read an important message from King John of Portugal.

The King asked Ignatius' help in finding priests to go to India to tell the people there everything about Christ, whom they did not know. Ignatius knew he must send Francis, who was his very best worker, and he was sad, knowing that he would probably never see him again in this life. "Go, Francis," he said with tears in his heart, "and set all on fire!"

Francis left for a three-month trip across the Alps and Spain to Portugal, where he would board a boat for the 11,000-mile voyage. He knew it would not be a short trip, but he never dreamed it would be 13 months! Can you imagine not walking on land or even seeing trees or houses for over a year?

The passengers and crew grew very restless. They were frightened, bored, grumpy and, most of all, sick. Most of them had scurvy, which came from eating poor food and not being able to have oranges and tomatoes and grapefruits. Vitamin C pills to take their place hadn't been invented yet. Francis did his best to soothe their fears, referee fights, tell them jokes and, through all of this, let them know that God was watching over them.

They finally arrived on the west coast of India in a town called Goa. Francis worked first among the rough and rude soldiers and colonists who had come from Europe and who no longer followed Christ's teaching. They were giving the native Indians a bad example of how Christians should act.

After convincing most of them to change their lives to let our Lord's light in, Francis went on to the southern coast and spent two years among the native pearl fishermen and their families. He lived as they did: slept on the ground, ate little but rice and water, washed his own clothes and cleaned his own pots. They loved him for this.

He had a funny way of getting people's attention in the villages where he preached. He would go through the streets ringing a little bell and, when the children and mothers came running, he would tell the story of our Lord and his mother in little rhymes, or fit the words to tunes, so they could hum them while they cut hay or mended nets. The little girls would jump rope as they sang:

Mary had a lit-tle Son,
lit-tle Son,
lit-tle Son,
Mary had a lit-tle Son,
Who came to save us all!

After traveling all over India teaching and baptizing, Francis set sail for the Spice Islands. He loved to offer Mass here, with the heavenly smell of cinnamon and nutmegs and cloves all about him to remind him of the sweetness of Christ's love for all his children. Then he set sail again, this time for Japan.

He found the people and their ways very different from those he had known in India. They did not seem friendly at all. Francis knew he must learn their language and learn it well. It took him a year before he felt sure enough of what he was saying. He certainly didn't want to offend a prospective Christian by calling him a cross-eyed porcupine when what he really wanted to say was, "How do you do, would you like to know how you can live forever?"

Even when he did learn to speak their tongue, the Japanese looked at him with scorn and then turned away so they wouldn't have to look at him at all. Francis sat down one day, scratched and bruised from stones thrown by children, and thought about this situation.

Why, he wondered, didn't he have the love and respect of these people as he did in India? Surely he was the same person. The

Holy Spirit gave him a nudge and something clicked in his understanding. The Japanese, being a very proud and respectable people, would not listen to a beggar who wore the same rags day after day, no matter what important message he brought.

He knew what he must do. He dressed in the most handsome robes he could find and, with his fellow priests in attendance like a royal procession, he presented himself to the ruler as a prince from Portugal. He gave the monarch an armful of gifts—a music box, a pair of velvet slippers, a cuckoo clock and a letter from King John, explaining who he was and why he was here.

The ruler was so pleased with this royal treatment he immediately gave the visitor permission to teach anywhere in his country and an old temple to live in. Once he had been accepted by them, Francis found the Japanese people to be gentle, gracious and nature-loving. They became Christians and friends. Often they asked him why he had come to Japan instead of China, since China was the most important "Forbidden Empire."

Francis felt it was time for him to go to China. But everything seemed to stand in his way. "You may be sure of one thing," he wrote to a friend, "the devil will be very sorry to see the Society of Jesus enter China, judging by the obstacles he puts in my way every day."

He persisted. Finally a friend told him of a Chinese pirate who would smuggle him into Canton. Francis waited for him on the hot, desolate, windswept island of Sanchian, off the China coast, for three months. But the pirate never came. Francis caught a fever and then a chill. He had wanted to get to China so badly, but our Lord must have felt that Francis had already done more than one saint should do. China must be left for the missionaries to come.

As he lay on the island shore in sand that burned his skin, he felt a touch cool as rainwater on his eyes. "Never mind, Francis," said a pleasant, pleased voice. "Think of all those happy people who know my Son because of you. Now don't fret over China. Just close your eyes, it's time to come home."

And he did.

PRAYER OF A WOULD-BE SAINT

with heart serene
and cheerful face
with will and wit
and God's good grace

let me
do what I can
where I am
with what I have